HANAHANA

HANAHANA

AN ORAL HISTORY ANTHOLOGY
OF HAWAII'S WORKING PEOPLE

Edited, with an introduction, by
MICHI KODAMA-NISHIMOTO
WARREN S. NISHIMOTO
CYNTHIA A. OSHIRO

Ethnic Studies Oral History Project,
University of Hawaii at Manoa
Honolulu

Library of Congress Cataloging in Publication Data

Kodama-Nishimoto, Michi, Warren S. Nishimoto, and Cynthia A. Oshiro
HANAHANA: An Oral History Anthology of Hawaii's Working People.

LOC 83–082457
ISBN 0–8248–0895–9

Royalties from the sale of this book will be used to
support further research and publication.

In memory of Koji Ariyoshi,
Hideo "Major" Okada
and John E. Reinecke
who dedicated their lives
to Hawaii's working people

Contents

Acknowledgments

We are indebted to the many individuals and organizations who have given us encouragement and assistance. Special thanks are extended to the following persons for reviewing sections of the manuscript: interviewers Ed Gerlock, Vivien Lee, Mark Matsunaga, Gael Gouveia Mustapha, Perry Nakayama; and interviewee family members Priscilla Meek, Merle Milles, Alberta Nakaima, and Mildred Takahashi. We also wish to thank Marie Hara, Arnold Hiura, Noel Kent, Franklin Odo, and Margaret Yamate for their helpful comments; L. Puaʻala Fisher, Nem Lau, Gale Yamada, and Henrietta Yee for administrative support; past and present advisory committee members (Diane Akau, Belinda Aquino, Edward Beechert, Stephen Boggs, Sabu Fujisaki, Robert Hasegawa, Carmen Oliveira, and Irma Soong) for their guidance; and the University of Hawaii Press staff, in particular Jan Heavenridge, Kathy Matsueda, and Iris Wiley, for their patience and expertise. In addition we acknowledge the Hawaii State Legislature which has supported this work through special appropriations to the State Foundation on Culture and the Arts. Finally, we wish to thank the twelve interviewees who so generously shared their lives with us.

Foreword

The men and women who speak to you through this book were in the prime of their lives between 1920 and 1960. In their own ways, they helped create the changes that saw Big Five control over Hawaii give way to multi-ethnic participation in a more democratic society.

HANAHANA: An Oral History Anthology of Hawaii's Working People brings the work of the Ethnic Studies Oral History Project (ESOHP) full circle. In 1976, collection of oral history interviews was the pressing objective. Funding was never secure, and we hoped for the opportunity to develop raw interviews into popular historical accounts about Hawaii's working people.

Several key people deserve special credit for the Project's success. Koji Ariyoshi, writer and social justice advocate, was the driving force and organizer behind the establishment of the ESOHP. His vision inspired our work. Hideo "Major" Okada, longtime labor and community activist, contributed his experience to nurture the project through difficult periods. John E. Reinecke, scholar and dedicated progressive, provided valuable historical insights based on his years of painstaking research into Hawaii's labor history. And, the ESOHP staff displayed its dedication and enthusiasm by continuing research and developing popular materials to increase our understanding of the people who helped make Hawaii what it is today.

I encourage your support for their efforts to continue this important work.

CHAD TANIGUCHI
ESOHP Principal Investigator,
1976–1983

Introduction

"On the plantation, morning time, *'Hoy, hanahana!'* See, even though
you tired. *'Hanahana!'* You got to work, . . . you know."
                                        —Severo Dinson, seventy-seven-
                                        year-old former plantation worker

Hanahana, a reduplication of the Hawaiian word, *hana,* is a pidgin
term for work. Originally used by immigrants who labored on the sugar
plantations, it later came to be used by other workers in Hawaii. The
term, as well as the hard work and way of life it connotes, transcended
ethnic and cultural barriers, providing people with a shared understanding of the work experience. Even today, older workers know and use the
term. Thus, the term's meaning, mixed origin, and common use by
workers make it an appropriate title for this ESOHP publication.

For the past seven years, the ESOHP, or Ethnic Studies Oral History
Project, has: 1) recorded and preserved interviews[1] with 250 of Hawaii's
working men and women who otherwise would not have left written
memoirs of their lives, and 2) distributed more than 10,000 pages of
verbatim transcripts[2] to the University of Hawaii and state regional
libraries. However, in their archival form, these tapes and transcripts
have not been fully utilized by students and the general public. The
sheer volume, lengthy question-and-answer format, and limited availa-
bility, have discouraged full use of the material. In view of this, the
need for a condensed, readable presentation that could be made easily
available to the public, was recognized. This book, *HANAHANA: An
Oral History Anthology of Hawaii's Working People,* was born out of
this need and ESOHP's commitment to recording and popularizing
working people's history.

The lives of working people in Hawaii's history—particularly that of
the twentieth century—have been long overlooked and until recently
taken for granted. This has been so largely because of:

1) the workers' lack of social prominence and the emphasis placed on the prominent and powerful by earlier writers,
2) the seeming sameness of day-to-day life, and the tendency for daily activities to fade against the backdrop of dramatic historic events,
3) the paucity of English-language materials written about and by workers, themselves, and
4) the absence of writers able to interpret the non-English materials (e.g., letters, diaries, songs based upon their experiences, vernacular newspapers, etc.) that do exist about native Hawaiian and immigrant workers.

Coming from non-English, semi-literate or non-literate backgrounds into work situations that afforded little time for reflection and writing, many workers were unable to record the details of life and work. Others with the requisite skills and time were not inclined to record their experiences or often lacked confidence in their abilities to do so. Then, too, few dreamt that their lives would someday be of historical interest. To many, like Lucy Robello, a plantation homemaker, everyday occurrences were of little significance:

C.T., ESOHP interviewer: See, there was a lot more that you remembered.
L.R.: Well, you asked me for it, so I had that to talk about. Otherwise, I don't think that was important at all. Is that important to you?
C.T.: Yeah, we trying to understand what went on back then.
L.R.: Oh. Because I don't see anything important in that. It was just a normal living . . .

It is only in retrospect, that historical significance has been attached to workers' lives like that of Lucy Robello. The achievements of common working people gained recognition and people's history gained credibility in the 1970s. What were formerly viewed as the routine activities of a "normal living" came to be seen as the workers' contributions to Hawaii's history. And, now as we begin to note changing lifestyles, the details of everyday life help define basic breaks and continuities from the past.

Fortunately, with the development of modern oral history and the statewide support given ESOHP during the past seven years, the life experiences of 250 working people have been preserved for posterity. Of this number, twelve are featured here in *HANAHANA,* an anthology of life narratives based on their oral history interviews.

The twelve, representing the values and lifestyles of different communities, are placed in four chapters. Ida Kanekoa Milles with her Hawaiian upbringing in isolated Nahiku, Maui, and Nelson Ah Hoy Chun, a rice and taro farmer in the Big Island's Waipio Valley, occupy Chapter I, "In the Country." Eleanor Heavey from Honolulu's tough working-class district, Kakaako, and Usaburo Katamoto who pursued boat building on the waterfront, follow in Chapter II, "In the City." Chapter III, "On the Plantation," features Lucy and Seraphine "Slim" Robello, a second-generation sugar plantation family; Adam Holmberg, locomotive brakeman; Cresencia and Pedro Ponce, participants in the 1924 Filipino Strike; and Emigdio Cabico, plantation store clerk. Violet Hew Zane, a storekeeper in Lower Paia, Maui, and Osame Manago, owner of a hotel in Captain Cook, Kona, Hawaii, occupy the concluding chapter, "In the Small Town."

While not wholly representative of the Islands' working people, these twelve do represent the best—or, at least a fraction of the best—of ESOHP's interviews. Many others could have been included in this volume, but limitations of time and space precluded their inclusion.

After a painstaking review and evaluation of the entire ESOHP collection, these twelve were selected for their portrayal of everyday life and work, their articulation of attitudes and feelings, and the documentation of major historical events as experienced and perceived by these individuals. Also considered in the selection process were the completeness and length of responses to the interviewer's queries, the interviewee's recall of events in a chronological sequence that lent itself to narrative treatment, and the interviewee's style of speech—with preference given to the more vivid, expressive speakers. It was also the editors' intent to have a variety of life and work experiences in different island localities and a number of Hawaii's major ethnic groups represented.

Following the selection process, the interviews were edited into coherent narratives. Ambiguous statements, interviewer's questions, and portions of dubious interest were removed and topics rearranged for readability and coherence. Added for fluidity were occasional conjunctive and transitional phrases; added for clarity were explanatory statements and definitions of non-English and other terms peculiar to Hawaii.

Although the editing process was unavoidably influenced by the editors' biases and judgments—just as the interviews were influenced by the interaction between interviewer and interviewee—particular attention was paid to the flavor and content of interviews and narratives. Following each interview and its editing into a narrative, interviewers and interviewees (or, their designated representatives) reviewed the materials. In addition, pre-interview documentary research,[3] the internal consistency of interview statements and the statements' concurrence with other sources were evaluated by editors. Every effort was made to verify information, but since these life histories portray personalities and events, many of which were of a personal nature and unverifiable due to the lack of corroborating documentation, readers should be aware of statements that may not be wholly factual. Even these statements, however, should not be summarily dismissed for they may yield valuable historical insights and convey ways people think about and remember the past.

Used with care and circumspection, *HANAHANA*'s twelve individual experiences can show us how some workers felt and lived, enrich our understanding of workers in twentieth-century Hawaii, and remind us that history is in the main about men and women like ourselves, who—when given a chance—can present their life stories with eloquence, understanding, and an unmatched sense of realism.

MICHI KODAMA-NISHIMOTO
WARREN S. NISHIMOTO
CYNTHIA A. OSHIRO
June, 1983

NOTES

1. Interview tapes are available for listening purposes at the Hawaiian and Pacific Collection (Hamilton Library, University of Hawaii at Manoa).

2. The transcripts are available in bound volumes under ESOHP authorship:
    Waialua and Haleiwa: The People Tell Their Story (Honolulu: ESOHP, 1977)
    Life Histories of Native Hawaiians (Honolulu: ESOHP, 1978)
    Waipi'o: Mano Wai (Source of Life) (Honolulu: ESOHP, 1978)
    Remembering Kakaako: 1910–1950 (Honolulu: ESOHP, 1978)
    The 1924 Filipino Strike on Kauai (Honolulu: ESOHP, 1979)
    Women Workers in Hawaii's Pineapple Industry (Honolulu: ESOHP, 1979)
    Stores and Storekeepers of Paia and Puunene, Maui (Honolulu: ESOHP, 1980)
    A Social History of Kona (Honolulu: ESOHP, 1981)
    Uchinanchu: A History of Okinawans in Hawaii, published by ESOHP in cooperation with the United Okinawan Association in 1981, also includes life history narratives based on oral history interviews with *issei,* first-generation Okinawans, who settled in the islands.

3. See introductory sections of ESOHP publications (cited in note 2) for further information on interview methodology and follow-up procedures.

Notes on Use

Brackets [ ] indicate statements added by the editors for clarification.

Italics denote non-English and onomatopoetic terms.

Names are rendered in Western style, given name preceding surname.

I
In the Country

Ida Kanekoa Milles
GETTING SOMEWHERES

ESOHP

Ida Kanekoa Milles was raised on Maui in the native Hawaiian lifestyle. Born in 1913, Ida's first language was Hawaiian. Her father was a taro grower; and her mother, a *lau hala* weaver.

Ida attended school in Nahiku village until the fifth grade. She was selected to go to Maunaolu Seminary where she stayed for a year until her father's illness forced the discontinuation of her studies. In 1927, Ida found her first job as a maid for a *haole* family in Kahului.

The following year, Ida married John Milles and gave birth to the first of her seven children. Ida, her husband and their eight-year-old son worked clearing land for Nahiku Ranch in the 1930s. Ida then did *hō hana,* or weeding, at Hana Sugar Plantation. Later, for extra money, Ida and her husband caught river shrimp which they sold to sugar plantation workers.

At the start of World War II, John Milles moved to Honolulu in search of work. Leaving the children with her mother, Ida followed, obtaining a job as a nursing home matron. In 1944, the Milleses bought a home and sent for their children. Ida then worked as a pantry woman at the USO (United Service Organizations), making salads and serving food to soldiers. At war's end, she became a school janitress, leaving in 1946 to work at the Hawaiian Pineapple Company (later called Dole Corporation) cannery.

Ida worked in the cannery preparation department, composed predominantly of women workers. The preparation department's hierarchical structure was based on differential status, pay and responsibility.

Trimmers, who removed blemishes from pineapples previously cored and peeled by a machine, and packers, who graded the pineapple slices and placed them in cans, wore and were called "white caps." Higher in rank were the "brown caps," or relievers, who substituted for white caps and aided the foreladies. Foreladies, or "blue caps," supervised the packers, trimmers and relievers. Above the foreladies were section heads, who assisted two head foreladies (one each for trimming and packing). In overall charge of the preparation department was a male superintendent.

Most of the cannery's full-time workers were men, who maintained the warehouses, ran the machinery, or supervised; while most of the part-timers were women, who worked mainly as trimmers and packers during the peak summer season.

Ida started as a trimmer and was eventually promoted to forelady. She retired in 1975, after thirty years of cannery work. She died five years later, at age sixty-seven.

Ida was interviewed twice in her Halawa Heights home by Michi Kodama-Nishimoto for a 1979 project, "Women Workers in Hawaii's Pineapple Industry." Michi, a researcher/interviewer, remembers Ida warmly, choosing the words "friendly, hospitable, open" to describe her. Ida was also very conscientious. Michi recalls in particular how Ida had stayed up late the night before the first interview session writing down her experiences in a notebook so that she would not forget anything important.

The narrative takes Ida from her childhood in an isolated rural village through her career in the pineapple cannery. Although she lived in a place and time of limited educational and occupational opportunities for women, Ida's strong desire to improve herself remained undiminished throughout her life. It is a recurring theme in her narrative.

IN MY YOUNGER TIME, I wanted to work. Yes, I do. I wanted to work, but like how you were telling that some women wants to be school-teacher, some wants to be nurse, I felt the same way. I like to have something that I can show my family, my children: what I was and how I get to show myself in my life. But some of the women tell you they couldn't afford school. That was the same like me. I couldn't afford it. I took all kinds of job because I didn't have much education to get the job that I wanted. But probably I might have gone to school when I was bearing my children. If my mind was strong at that time, maybe I would go back to school and get back the things that I want. But I didn't.

My young time, I want to be a schoolteacher, but my parents couldn't afford. I attended the school in Nahiku until fifth grade. After fifth grade I couldn't afford to go to Hana School because we have no transportation. My parents were poor. I stayed home helping them. Then the principal from Maunaolu Seminary came to that little village in Nahiku. She found some students. I was one of them. She talked it over with my parents but, to tell you the truth, my parents don't understand English. They understands only Hawaiian language, and we children answered them back in Hawaiian. We don't dare answer them back in English because we going get it from them. Anyway, as she was talking, I translated into the Hawaiian language. My father said, "I think I could. I'll pay." The tuition in those days was cheap. He could afford to pay for my school if I want to go. I do really wanted an education. I went to Maunaolu Seminary and stayed for a year. I came back. My father took ill and I couldn't go back to school.

I was sad. I wish I could get a job. In that village, job was very scarce—you can't find any job unless you work in the sugar plantation. To get to the plantation, you have to have transportation. But we couldn't afford it. There's no way to come and get you because as you traveling to Hana, you have to leave the main highway and go three miles down. That's where Nahiku Village is.

That's where I was born in the island of Maui . . . May the fourth, 1913. And I remember my father, my mother and I and my little brother at this little village. We travel by foot to go there and live. My father builds a grass shack. I lived in that kind of house. Nothing on the floor, just a dirt. My mother used to weave about three or four mats to lay on the ground. That's our bed. My brother and I were the only children that lives there. I enjoy living there because fruits were plentiful. Lots of bananas and sugar cane—it grows wild—and lots of passion fruit. You know those purple ones? Where we live they have spring water and the water flow freely. I go to the river to catch shrimps and I enjoy it. Lots of wild goldfish, too. Just for the fun of it, we used to catch and put it in a bottle, just to admire it. My brother and I enjoy it very much. Those days, I wasn't afraid of nothing because nobody would harm you. The place were wilderness with nobody around.

I remember my father was a hardworking man. He tried to do what he could to keep his family. My father and mother travel about five miles to the beach and catch *'opihi*s, go fishing. My father plants taro for our own use. Taro, watermelon, corn, sweet potato, cabbage, cucumber, all those things that the family need. My mother sells hats to buy the other things that we need. In those days, salt, sugar, flour and *shōyu,* that would be enough. And my father traveled to a little town —called Hana—to buy our groceries. He didn't return in the evening because he travels on a donkey. My father works for the County of Maui three days a week—cutting grass by the side of the road, cutting guavas, cutting trees. In those days, wages were very little, about five dollars a week, but the food was cheap, too. So it wasn't too bad.

I helped my mother gather *lau hala,* the dry *lau hala. Lau hala*s just fall on the ground and you pick up whatever you want. And I helped her up in the mountain to get bamboo for hats. My mother and I bring the bamboo home and cut it into three layers until we get to the soft tissue. We boil the water, roll the bamboo into a ball, and put it in the boiling water for about fifteen minutes. We take it out and bleach it out in the sun. That's the thing she makes hat with. It's a beautiful white hat. I helped my mother do all these things; even though it wasn't easy for me.

Even when I started working, whatever I earned, I give it to my parents. After I didn't go back to school, my parents decide to move to Kahului. When they move over there, my father wasn't working. My parents were living with an uncle and an aunt. That time . . . I didn't care to work as a maid but I think that is the only kind of a job that I know. Any other job I wouldn't know. So because I needed a job I worked there 1927 in the month of March.

This *haole* couple have two children. The mother comes here to Honolulu on business; the father was a banker. I takes care of the children. Just like a governess wherever they go, I goes with them.

I live there. I have my own cottage. I work continuously. You see, morning we get up at seven o'clock. We have our breakfast, then they both goes to work. Then I send the two children to school. While I was working, I wanted to go back to school, but the maid pay was very little. Twenty-one dollars a month. So I stay home take care of the house and take care whatever I have to do.

Mrs. Patterson, the wife, plans all the meals. The meals were very simple: a hamburger, a vegetable, mashed potato, slice of bread, milk. It was a simple thing to learn to make a hamburger. Sometimes, Mrs. Patterson writes the meals down and place it on the kitchen wall. Then she tells me, "Ida, this is the meal I want you to prepare. . . . " She stay overnight in Honolulu. Then I prepared the meal. It was a good thing that I learned how to read and how to write because I was young to accept that job—I was only thirteen years old!

Because I was young, I class myself just like a child, too. I loved to do things with the children. Especially when they comes home from school, and we get together. We play together in the yard, or gather eggs together and take it to the store. This couple, they were good to me. They help me, and I learn a lot from them, also.

They teach me how to cook. They teach me table manners. They teach me about some school things—arithmetic and geography, and many other things. They teach me how to speak. They teach me how to wash white things with Chlorox. They have washing machine. I didn't know how washing machine look like. Before, my mother and I wash our clothes in the river. White clothes, we have to soap it and bleach it out in the sun. Working as a maid, I learn how to use Chlorox and many other things. Those things, I learn lot of them there.

But to tell you the truth, at the beginning, I didn't like the job. Because they were white people, I felt uncomfortable. Before, they were so rare—I mean, rare, those kind of people. Only when I moved to Kahului, I seen lot of *haoles*. I seen Chinese, Japanese, too. But where we were living before, we didn't have those kind of nationalities. You see. Where I live, in that village, even when the airplane flies over, it was something unusual! When it flies over, we look at that and say, "What is this?" When we see white people come, they cover their faces with handkerchief. We wonder why. I admire these white people. They're so white and good-looking. I used to ask my parents, "Why, why do they cover (laughs) their face?" You see how ignorant we were. You know, when I thinking now, I says, "Oh, what a life." I think just like we were hillbilly or something. Oh, we were in the Dark Age, eh? But this *haole* couple, they were wonderful.

Until November the third, I think, I stayed over there. Then my parents wants to go back home. I didn't want to leave Kahului, but I still wasn't old enough to go on my own. Besides, I love my parents. They were old. So, I went back to Nahiku in 1927. I think in the month of December. Then I married young—very young, when I was fifteen.

First two years in my marriage, I didn't do anything. I stayed home take care my children. My first son, John [Milles, Jr.] was born November 21, 1928. My second child, Ida K. Milles, January 25, 1931. In between they were two years apart. Then my third child, Margaret, she born February 10, 1932. From Margaret to Margorie, they were a year apart. In 1934, between Margorie and George Milles, I have a little boy, Peter Paul. But he died in the age of eight. My fifth child, George, was born December 17, 1936. Then after that I have another child, Barbara, born January 25, 1939. I wasn't working, but I started to work when my first child was eight years old.

My husband was working for the WPA [Works Progress Administration]. He works for Nahiku Ranch as part-time. The ranch pays him only one dollar a day. The foreman hires lots of workers. He says, "If you really want to work, you can work for the ranch."

I cook lunch for my husband and son, then take to the pastures where they work. My son, only eight years old, works in the ranch—cutting those guavas and all that. I say, "If my son could do that, I could do it, too." So I start working.

Working on the ranch wasn't hard. To me, just like how I clean my yard. That's the way I was doing. Cutting the guava trees. I use a cane knife to cut the trees down. Lantana—I cut it to clear the pastures. I was working with my son, my husband, and other workers of the ranch. Oh! We talked, we laughed, yeah. And maybe there's certain trees I cannot cut, I call my husband to do it for me, and if he's not there, I see the nearest man—I call him to do it. (Laughs) You have to get the manpower to do it. And the boss of the ranch, he doesn't bother. He gives the order, "You clean this section up." If you finish, he comes, look, and that's it. He don't bother you. But you want to be honest, you do an honest job. And to me, I think it doesn't matter if it's a man or woman job. It's all up to you how you accepted it.

But, later, well, I just get tired of—(laughs).

My husband just tells me, "Enough working for you. You stay home."

I say, "What am I working for? Everything is cheap and my husband have enough to support us." So, I quit. I stayed home.

Next, well, just curiosity. I start working Hana Sugar Company. Lots of women work in the plantation. They have Japanese, they have Filipinos, but I'm the only Hawaiian. I worked there because my niece used to work. She and I go work together. When I first started, it was really hard for me. I have to know how to hold my hoe, how to get the weeds out. I have to learn. Then it was easy. I get acquainted with others, and it gets the job very interesting. That's what I want. I like to meet people, talking with them.

It was enjoyable working. No matter where I work, I make friends. I made friends with these ladies; we all worked together. Then, if I get through first and see that person have couple more rows, I go there and give them a hand. Of course, I don't have to help the next person, but it's better to help each other. So everybody can go home together.

After two or three summers, well, I stop. My husband tells me, "Stay home. I don't want you to go work in the plantation field anymore. Enough working for you. You learn enough and what I'm earning is enough."

You see, my young days, no person better than you. Everybody's the same. We don't have that kind of competitive people. We live among Portuguese people who own a lot of ranch property, cattle. We live on the ranch and had a pretty good life. I mean, the house were rent-free and we do what we want. Only what we have to do is to furnish. We didn't have fabulous furnitures. We just have couple chairs and beds. But, with whatever we have, we're satisfied.

So, I stayed home to raise my children, and in between 1936 and 1941, we used to go catch wild shrimps in the river and sell. On Saturdays, my husband sell and with the money, he used to buy dresses for the children, clothes for myself and him, or something that we need. But he didn't buy sheets or underwear. We used rice bag, flour bag sheets. We used to bleach 'em out in the sun, make it white. Sew panties for the children; make shirts for the men.

Then in 1941. Here I goes again, go back to my old hometown in Nahiku and stay there with my mother. We left the ranch and went back there to stay.

Then the war break out. My husband wasn't working at that time, so my brother who was in Honolulu asked him to come. My husband came and stayed with my brother. He got a job in Fort Armstrong. But, during the war, they wasn't paying very good, just seventy-five cents an hour.

And then, I came here to visit, and this woman offer me a job as a matron. I think to myself, "Shall I accept the job?" I was worried about my children back home. I have to ask my mother if she could take care my children. I went back to Maui and asked my mother if I could accept this job. She says, "Go right ahead. I'll take care of the children." So, I left my children there.

I felt so sad leaving my mother and my children back home. But, my mother encourage me and says, "I think if you go to work and help your husband, you won't come back to this life again. Maybe you will make better of life." So, I took her word for it.

I thought I may be able to get somewheres. I'm that kind of woman, I like to improve myself. I been living in Nahiku so long, I guess I'm tired of that life. I haven't been out in the world to see how other people live. I live in that little village, getting married, and raising my children. I think maybe this is my chance to prove to myself that I have something to live with. So, I accepted that job.

I came back to Honolulu and worked at that place until 1944. I work and sent money home. I tell my mother, "Don't you do anything in the yard. Don't you plant anything. Just take care of yourself. Tell the children to take care the yard. You buy your *poi*." My mother was old and I didn't want her to work hard. And every three months, my husband and I goes back home.

In Honolulu where I was a matron, I used to take care three women. Take care their clothing, bathe them, feed them, take them to a doctor. That's the kind of work I was doing, and the pay was pretty good. I get paid by every other week. It was forty dollars, I think. Forty dollars. My other jobs, I didn't receive that much money. To me, I was happy to get that much. I really enjoyed that job because I take care these old ladies and I learn a lot from them, also. They talk to me about their childhood time and how they go through with their life. These people are *haole* people and, sometimes, I listen to them, I feel so sad of their life. But, I learn, learn a lot from them until 1944.

That time, I told my husband, "Daddy, I don't want to go back to Maui." He wants to go back. He loves that life. I said, "No. I don't want to go back." To tell you the truth, I begged him. I says, "I don't want to go back to that life again." Nobody would improve themselves there. They live day in and day out the same way.

He say, "What are you going to do?"

I said, "The savings that we have, I'm going to buy a home."

He told me, "You think Mother would like to come here and live?"

I told him, "She will."

So we took all our savings out and bought this home on School Street. It was not a new home—it was twelve years old, I think. But was cheap—$6,000. To put down (i.e., to make a down payment) was $2,500. Then, I furnish. I found this place where they were selling secondhand furnitures. So I bought and furnished my living room, my bedrooms, my kitchen. I was satisfy.

I went back to Maui and brought my mother and children. When I returned from Maui, my head matron told me the old ladies, the family are taking over. They don't have to hire anybody to take care of them. Well, I really felt disappointed. After I was laid off, I start looking for another job.

Then, I met a friend. She tells me, "Ida, you want to work at the USO (United Service Organizations)?"

"What doing?" I told her.

She says, "Pantry woman. You make salad and prepare other kinds of food."

I says, "Okay."

So, I start working in there as a pantry woman. The pantry is downstairs. Then, they put me upstairs to serve on the counter, where all the service boys comes in to have lunch. That, serving the men, I don't like. (Laughs) Sometimes the service boys get into my nerve. They like to give wisecrack or do something that I don't like, eh. Sometimes I serve them, they tells, "I didn't order this. We not going to eat this food." Other times they call, "Hey, lady, how about a date. Hey, lady, what are you doing tonight?" All those things. We married ladies shouldn't work in that kind of place. Maybe for single girls, all right.

Anyway, I associate with lot of people, all kinds. I associate with those rough ones; learn of different attitudes. I worked for couple months. Then, the war ended. When the USO shut down, I have to look for another job.

I heard they were hiring a matron to work in Kauluwela School. I went to the principal's office and asked if I could apply. She told me, "Okay, you can have the job. But when you come in, you have to fill up a form." I fill it up, and then she told me, "You come in seven o'clock in the morning. I tell you. I show you." She told me what to do as a matron. It's not a matron like, but just like a janitress: taking care her office, and seeing that the children keep the restroom clean. That's the kind of job I was working. I don't care for that job, but I have to help my husband meet the note of our home. So, when I meet the house payment, I quit. I worked there only about four months, I think. Then, I went hunting job in the pineapple cannery.

I met some friends. They said, "Because cannery has lot of women workers you enjoy working, lots of fun." That's the reason why I went work in the cannery. I started work 1946. The cannery name was Hawaiian Pine. It wasn't called Dole yet. I went to the employment office at Hawaiian Pine and one Mr. Chang hires whoever wants to work. Well, when I went there, he hired me. My niece was a trimmer. She told me, "Auntie, I think it's better for you to be a trimmer because trimming, you just pick up your pine [pineapple]. You don't have to know the difference between the fruit. Like packing pine slices, they have so many things to learn." So, I decide to take trimming.

Well, when they hired me as a trimmer, I didn't have any idea that it's going to be hard, or I'm going to be wet with juice on my apron. To tell you the truth, I sat on that table and looking at the pineapple com-

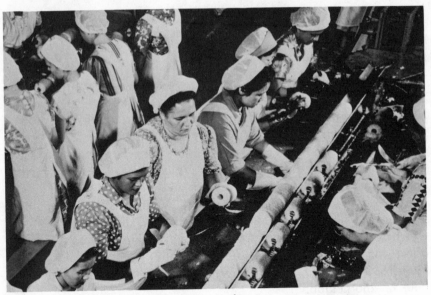

Pineapple trimmers, c. 1950s. *Hawaii State Archives*

ing through the Ginaca [machine that cores and skins pineapples] to me look like 100 pineapples a minute. Before I finish one pine, there's another one coming down. I put this pine down, I pick up another. I didn't finish, another pine coming down. Before I realize, there was a pile of fruit in front of me.

Forelady realize that I was in trouble. She asked, "Ida, what's the matter?"

I told her, "I don't know. I can't keep up with these pineapples."

She take the pine, saying, "Turn this way. You count one, and two." You see, one, and two knife strokes. Then you turn on the other side of the pineapple and do the same thing. If you see that the pineapple is all clean, then you put it in the chain [conveyor] and let it go to the packing table.

The forelady taught me how to trim faster. And the girls that I worked with helps me trim my fruit. That's the important thing. Working on the table, helping one another. As we talk, our hands still moving, trimming the pines. We talking about our life. We telling each other where we were born, what kind of a life we had, how many children we had, and what school did we go to. Either my neighbor tells me her life story, or I tells her mine. The time go fast. We keep talking or sing. That's to not get bored, trimming only.

I became expert in trimming. I work about three years at the cannery.

The head forelady calls me into the office and ask me if I want to accept a reliever position. I say, "I want to try." I like to improve myself to see if I can learn something new, not to be a trimmer, a white cap, all the time. So I was promoted to brown cap—that's a reliever. When a girl goes out to the restroom or wherever, the reliever takes over her place to trim. If nobody goes out, the reliever assist the forelady. When the summer night shift workers comes in and everyone is new, the relievers help train them. Some of the new girls quickly get emotional. You have to have patience—patience in everything that you do.

To me, this position as trimming reliever is harder than trimming. But I like it because it shows I improve myself. I enjoy the changing of cap, more responsibility and more money.

Then another position was open as a labor quota, so I try this position. I was labor quota for trimming side, and another girl was labor quota on packing side. In the morning when the workers come in, our work is to count the whole cannery. If we are short of workers, then we have to borrow. Either the packing side borrow from our side to go and fill up their side, or we borrow from packing side to come to the trimming side. So labor quota control the Preparation Department—packing and trimming. It's pencil work. I have to remember the quota of girls: how many are going home, and how many are working. It has to be counted correctly; all the reports has to go in the main office. My brains work hard. But, to choose between this and other jobs, I would rather have labor quota. No pineapple to trim, I'm clean all day. But the pay wasn't as good as forelady pay.

So, in 1950, when the head forelady tells me, "You be forelady for the night shift," I accepted. Oh, I feel proud. I feel happy because that shows I'm really improving my job to have that position. The pay was better and the cap was different, too. Forelady is a blue cap. I'm responsible for fourteen to twenty-four girls. I have to watch that the girls are doing the proper way: handling, trimming, and putting their fruit on the chain.

But that wasn't my first experience to be a forelady. You see, the union [International Longshoremen's and Warehousemen's Union] came to the cannery in 1946. Then, in 1947, they strike. All the union members stayed out. My daughter was working in the cannery that time, too. She and I seen this picket line. We stand and wonder, "What's going on?"

The cannery foreman come across and call out, "Who wants to work?"

I step out and say, "I want to work." I want the money. If I stay home, no income. So my daughter and I follow the foreman through the picket line.

When I went down to the table, there wasn't no foreladies. Only the scabs like me, few other workers. Because some old-time foreladies were officers for the union, we were short of foreladies. So I became a forelady without training.

First day of the strike, my daughter and I go to work. Second day, my daughter did not go to work with me. She was afraid. But I went in. She says, "How did Mama get the nerve to go work." But it doesn't bother me. I went to work every day.

But the strike did not last long [five and a half days]. When it was over, the regular foreladies went back to their own positions. I was demoted to white cap. There was some ill feeling the strikers had against us because we kept going to work instead of stay home. Cold shoulder, whisper that I was one of the scabs. So, instead of staying there and be miserable—working with them, not happy—I didn't go back to work. Then, I think to myself, "Go back again to the cannery." The old workers changed their attitude so I went back in 1948.

Forelady job, it's not easy. When the union came in, anything wrong that the foreladies or head foreladies do, the workers turn 'em into the union. So, the foreladies and head foreladies have to treat the girls right. And the union asking for more wages. So then I guess the company stop giving all those free things, like free lunch and parties for the children at Christmas time. Oh, we feel sad because the company don't treat us any more free things. But what can we do? So we all went without those things. And that's when the company start putting more rules in. You cannot sing or talk too much on the table. You have to be very serious on your job. They start coming and checking how you trim. So the foreladies and relievers on their toes, keeping their eyes on the workers.

But you have to give and take. You cannot be too strict on the girls because they won't cooperate if you are hard on them. This supervisor, Dee Dupont, who worked in the main office [in the late 1950s], was giving orders. You have to trim your pineapple this way and that way. You have to stand right in back of the girls when you write your tally cards [to record the number of spoiled pineapples thrown away by the trimmers]. The girls didn't like that. It was hard on the girls, and hard on the foreladies to do that. So the women decided to walk out because they couldn't take it. Six hundred women walk out [for one day in 1957].

But I didn't want to walk out. Of course, they're going to tell me that

I'm a company lady, but it's not that. I'm working there, and if they give me that rule, no matter where I work, I just follow the rule. When the people came back, they said, "Why didn't you walk out?"

I says, "If she's the head and tells me that's the way to do it, I do it."

Even though I didn't walk out that time, I really had good relationship with my fellow workers and foreladies. They choose me as union steward in 1960. The steward takes all the rap. The girls telling, "Oh, the pineapple is coming out so fast," and, "This head forelady, oh, she scold me." All these things, we have to go in and face the company and tell the condition of the job. But before we face them, we have to know what's wrong. We call an appointment with the foreman or superintendent. They come in, sit down and talk. Then, some problems that we take in, it's solved. That's one thing I give credit to the union. It humbles the management.

But when the union strike, it's hard for the women. I think the only job they know is the cannery. That's where the bread and butter comes in. Like myself, my husband was working for the government. He take care of me. But it was terrible for the women who doesn't have any husband or other help.

To tell you the truth, I didn't like to strike. I didn't strike the first time, but since I joined the union I have to help them picket during the 1968 and 1974 strikes. They choose me as captain. I have so many girls with me. We stand picket. The union were supplying them with food, but no money comes in. So we all lost out when we strike.

One year after the 1974 strike, I retire at sixty-two. I think, that's enough. I was tired of working. When you retire from the cannery, they give you a lump sum. Some retirees have $5,000, $6,000. But how long that money going to last? The only other benefit you have is your Social Security. If you work other jobs, maybe you get good retirement, but not the pineapple cannery.

That's the only reason why I don't want my children to be employed in the cannery. When my daughter were there, she was well liked by all the section heads, the head foreladies, the workers. But she wanted to improve herself, so she quit the cannery and got another job. I'm not telling you cannot make your life with the cannery, but I didn't want my children to work all their lifetime there.

But me, I enjoy working in all the job I been doing. My ambition was I want to work to earn and learn. To feel that you earn your own money and know that you worked for it. That's the feeling I have. My working life, I have no complaint.

Nelson Ah Hoy Chun
NATURE'S WORK

Hin Chun, Nelson Chun's father, immigrated to Hawaii from China in circa 1895. For two years, Hin Chun worked at Paauilo Sugar Plantation on the Big Island's Hamakua Coast. Later, he and his wife joined other Chinese laborers who moved to Waipio Valley to farm rice.

Nelson, born on June 18, 1900, in Waipio, helped in his father's rice fields after school and on weekends. In 1922, Hin Chun died and Nelson took over the fields.

Because of heavy competition from California-grown rice and the difficulties in cultivating and harvesting the crop, Waipio's farmers gradually converted their fields to taro, the staple of the Hawaiian diet. Nelson harvested Waipio's last rice crop in 1928. Since then, he has farmed taro despite numerous setbacks such as the 1946 tidal wave that destroyed his home and crops. This incident, along with floods, crop disease, and the desire of Waipio's young people to seek greater educational and job opportunities in towns and cities, caused an exodus from the valley. What was once a valley of hundreds is now home for less than fifty. Most of the surviving taro farmers commute to the valley, still accessible only by jeep, from the nearby towns of Kukuihaele and Honokaa.

In the 1950s, Nelson, his wife (whom he married in 1924), and four children moved out of the valley into a house he built in Honokaa. Today, he drives daily into the valley to tend his taro, lotus, and water chestnuts.

Interviewer Vivien Lee interviewed Nelson in 1978, along with thirty-two other present and former residents of Waipio to gather information on: the taro-growing process; the relationships among farmers, residents, and taro processors; the economic factors involved in farming taro; and the lifestyle that evolved in the valley. Nelson's interview is notable not only for its wealth of detailed information on the subjects, but also for its first-person description of hard work, independence, and one man's challenge to nature's destructive power.

Vivien also was impressed with the person himself. Shortly after her first meeting with Nelson, Vivien recorded, "Mr. Chun is a slight man —one of his eyes is almost closed. He's had two operations on it already. But he has a good memory. He is so animated and energetic, it is infectious. He has an aliveness about him—and he is seventy-eight years old!"

A FARMER has to rely on nature. That's my policy. Nature not with you, you just out of luck. One disease can sweep you clean, one flood can sweep you clean. It's just nature's work. How you going stop? It's just impossible to stop. If you lose one crop, it takes you two, three crops to get back to your feet.

You know what I mean by losing? One time, after my father and his workers harvested the rice, one flood come down, sweep 'em. After one whole day cutting, the flood take the rice all away. What can you do? Just drop tears, that's all. Somebody asked me one time, "What if human being do that?"

I said, "I shoot that fellow down."

I realized my father was a rice farmer when I was a small kid, about six years old, when we were working in our farm together. But all that time, when you small, you don't take notice of what the parents doing.

He came down Waipio to start a rice farm around the late 1890s. Before that, I really don't know what he did in China. Must be he rice farmer. They get just small portion. In China hard to own plenty land, you know. You had to be rich to own plenty.

In my early days, rice farming was done by hand: planting, harvesting, everything. Plowing, you use two horses and two people manage the team. One is the driver and one holds the plow. And you have to harrow three, four times before you can break up the soil. Then you have to prepare seed beds where you want the rice seedlings to start. You try and plant in the high place where floods doesn't catch. Of course, when Waipio floods, our section always catch. Get real big

Waipio Valley rice fields, 1924. *Courtesy Bishop Museum*

water. So, planting's really not easy work, you know. Even harvesting is hard work. You start in the morning. Half an hour after that you get all soaked wet.

But the worse job when I was small was scaring away the rice birds. We built a tower from twelve to sixteen feet above the ground. It had a platform to sit down on. And get ten, fifteen lines of string, all come to the tower. You strip cloth rags—you tie on. And get the five-gallon kerosene can at the end and drop four or five *kukui* nut in there. Every time you pull the string, the rags going shake. The birds scared, eh. And that noise from the cans—the birds get scared, fly away.

So from morning time, as soon as dawn, you there on the platform. And you don't get your breakfast until somebody come relieve you. You go home, eat, and come back again. Pretty soon the birds go into the guava and they watch. Little by little, they try to sneak into the rice field. So you have to be wide awake and keep on shaking the can. Otherwise they be eating before you know it.

Sometimes, no matter how you try, they won't fly away. One time they got me so mad I went home, get the twelve gauge, and *wen* try blow 'em down.

But still yet they come. They have time to fill their stomachs before they go home to nest. Just before dark you see them going. Hoo, by the thousands! In the morning you see them swooping down—airplane is not as fast.

Even after the rice was harvested and bundled up, birds used to come and eat. So I grab my net, go sneak around from behind and throw the net right over, catch 'em. One crack, 600, 700, 800 birds.

And we eat 'em! Good-eating birds, you know. But to clean 'em, ah, that's not easy job. You de-feather, but don't skin 'em. You skin 'em, doesn't taste good because the fat on the skin. Cut the heart, throw 'em out. Cut 'em open from the back, take off the guts, wash everything. My brother, Ah Kong, was fast with his fingers. He could clean two, three; we cannot clean one. Even my mother cannot beat him. Then you face 'em down on the chopping board and just slap 'em with *da kine* Chinese knife. You smash the bones; they come flat.

Then you get *shōyu*, salt, little bit sugar, and marinate that for an hour or so. Dip that bird in egg batter and deep fry the thing. The big bone you cannot eat, but the small bones, you can chew 'em. You ever try that, boy, you won't eat any other birds.

My father subleased the rice land from a Chinese man, Akaka. Leong Kut is his regular name, but Hawaiians called him Akaka. He owned a store and a rice mill. My father and other growers respected him because he was kind enough to give them food and pay the workmen and everything. Then Akaka have to wait to get his money back. You go to his store and instead of paying cash, you charge until the crop comes. According to my father, Akaka make so much profit on his groceries compared to other stores.

And all the Waipio rice goes to Akaka, because that was the only rice mill. He buy rice from the growers, mill himself, and sell the milled rice. He makes that much profit again.

So we had to get good crops every year to pay our debts. My father hired a few Chinese men for harvesting and planting. That's the only time they get work. You know, had six or seven big rice companies down in Waipio that hired Chinese to work. The big one, they call Hui Nui. *Hui* is "company," *nui* is "big." Harvest time and plant time they hire a lot of people.

I used to plant rice for the Hui Nui. The day I didn't go to work, they had to put three fellas in my place. They were paying workers one dollar a day. But you know how much they pay me? Only fifty cents a day.

So the next crop come, they ask me for work again. My father say, "You're not going. Why should you be going? You more than double their work and they pay you only half a dollar. The other fellas so slow."

They say to my father, "Yeah, but he's only a boy—only twelve years old."

So I tell 'em, "My father say I'm not going work. He says stay home, cut grass, feed the horses."

The men Hui Nui hired lived in rough lumber buildings. Wooden shingle roofing; no ceiling. Maybe five, six—all single men—in one house. They don't have rooms. It was just like one big hall with beds.

You know their beds? Each bed is just a board placed on top two wooden horses. That's all they get. On the board, they get only straw mat. Hard to sleep, you know. It's all right if you sleep only on your back. But when you like move sideways it's hard; catch the hip bone, eh?

Some of them, during free time, smoked opium. That thing is more expensive than gold, and yet they smoke. Smells real good, you know. But I haven't tried. I don't want to. I think they smoked once a day, evening time. When they don't have that they look more like one dope, more like half-dead. After they smoke, they come real lively, you know.

During our time when we get rice fields, had plenty Chinese in Waipio. Eight or nine times a year we have a party together on holidays like the Moon Festival, Chinese New Year, and July 14—Chinese call it Chut Gnit Sup See. We cook Chinese dinner: chicken, duck, chop suey, some kind of fish, some kind of vegetables. You get about seven, eight kind stuff on the table.

And we went up to the Chinese temple and pray. First, we set the incense, then the candle. Then we place the tea and liquor. Then we put pork, chicken, fish, vegetables, orange, and eggs. No beef, though. That's one thing we don't use. Afterwards we take 'em home, eat 'em. People say the spirits already eat. But, how can you tell if they eat or not? That's one thing I cannot see. You know, sometimes I think it's only superstitious.

But I tell you one story. This was after my father died. My mother, one time, tell me, "Gee, last night I dreamed Father came back. He says somebody *wen* rob him, broke his house. Ah Hoy, you go up to the grave, see if there's anything wrong over there."

I went up there, look. Yes, must be something wrong.

You see, one old man just died. Andoi, my friend, buried that old man right next to my father. So I ask, "Eh, Andoi. When you bury that old man over there, you never broke anything?"

"No."

"You never find board or anything?"

"Yeah, one piece board like this long."

You see, my father get double coffin. One inside, one outside. Andoi *wen* bust the outside coffin.

I said, "Redwood?"

"Yeah."

"You bust the coffin of my father."

So I call up Dr. Carter. He was taking care of the cemetery. I tell, "Eh, Dr. Carter. You give Andoi the stiff for bury, eh?"

"Yeah."

"He bury old man right next to my father's grave and bust the outside coffin. I going move the grave."

So I go get one crowbar. I stuck the bar inside. Keep on pushing until the coffin move off. Set 'em back. The ground is soft yet.

You see, that's the one thing. I don't believe in dreams and everything, yet that dream was true. I tell my mother, "Funny. Father died so many years ago and still yet he said that it's his house."

My father passed away in 1922, and I took over the rice fields until 1928. That was my last rice crop. California rice was wholesaling for $2.90 and it cost us $4.50 to produce a bag. Doesn't pay. But that's not the only reason I quit.

If you plant rice, flood come down. Mud going cover up so much of the rice, it going slow the growth. And after the rice grown, you will have more stalk than seed so you don't get many grains on one plant.

Another way you lose is when the rice is nearly ripe and the wind or rain come. The wind going knock the seeds off the plant. And if heavy rain come, it's hard to harvest. Instead of picking two at a time, you have to pick one at a time.

Geez, when it rains, your heart pounds; when it winds, your heart pounds. Just keep pounding. I thinking, gee, how much am I going to lose? That's why I wouldn't go into rice again, never! You think the one who finance you is going to pity you? You pay for what you borrow.

So after 1928, I went all into taro. Taro is easier than rice. It's not as hard on the back. Rice, you have to plow every time and harrow and then plant. But taro, all you do is harrow. You don't have to plow. Once you get the patches ready for planting, you don't have much trouble.

I learned about taro because I used to pull taro for the fun of it. A big Hawaiian fellow by the name of Tom Kua would lift two bunch taro and swing 'em on top the shoulder. Some strong fellows can carry taro like that. The other farmers kidded me, "I like see the rice farmer do like Tom did."

So I stay with them and learned little by little. I got my *huli*, or plantings from other farmers. You pull and take what you can pull. Some farmers, nice. Sometimes they pity us, give us a few bundles of *huli*.

Then, I learned the value of fertilizer. The University of Hawaii Extension people came up and say, "You fertilize, you get more taro."

I say, "Yeah, well, we'll go try."

Sure enough, you know. One time, I went up to this old-timer's place to make seed, or cut *huli*, and he said, "Where you can find taro get five or six *keiki*, or shoots, on one plant? Only I get."

I said, "Five, six *keiki* is easy. I get some with ten."

"Oh, how can you tell me such a lie? I was born and raised in a taro patch. I like see your taro."

I said, "Okay, someday you come down and I show you the patch."

Sure enough, one day he come down early Sunday morning.

I said, "You want to drink coffee?"

"No, no, I not going drink coffee yet. I like see your taro. You remember you told me you get more than ten *keiki*?"

"Sure, I'll show you." So we walked. "In this patch. Go feel the taro."

When he feel 'em, he said, "That's the first time in history. How do you get ten *keiki*?"

It was actually the fertilizer, but I say to him, "I don't know. Maybe nature gave me that much." (Chuckles)

Not only fertilizer, but we rely on the water, too. You know, there are disadvantages and advantages. If the flood doesn't catch 'em so often, the taro grow all the time, big and heavy. But if flood catch 'em all the time, all the leaves drop off and the taro won't grow so big.

Taro is something funny. More sun and less rain is better. Some fellow tell me, "*Shee,* all dry spell. I bet it affect your taro."

I say, "No, the taro grow better." Because water is running through the patches all the time anyway.

The worst thing today is the disease, taro rot. We cannot tell how good our crop is, and how much we going get out of it. The University cannot help us. They never did give us a satisfactory answer. The taro sometimes rot and you have to chop 'em down.

All depends on nature, that's all. You can't fight it.

One of my biggest loss was on April Fools' Day, 1946. Our taro was real big, six or seven pounds, ready for harvest. After breakfast two of my workmen and I went up to a taro patch about 300 yards from my house. Around seven o'clock in the morning, my wife blew the horn, it means emergency.

So, I tell them, "Gee, what's wrong?" I stood up from where I was pulling taro and looked down toward the beach. I saw the water going over the river banks. I knew was tidal wave.

Waipio Valley taro patch, 1978. *ESOHP*

So, I tell my workmen, "Let's go home." One man followed me back, but the other one went up the valley instead. Then just before I reached the house, I saw the patch I just planted. I noticed the waves took off all the young taro already.

But whenever we had tidal waves before, they just come one or two or three waves at the most, see. Nothing serious. So when I look at all the fish, *ulua,* cutting the water in the taro patch, I tell my wife, "I'm going to get my net and catch some fish."

She said, "You better watch out."

So I get my net ready and watched the fish. The water is so dirty; the fish cannot see, almost blind. I said to the fish, "As soon as you hit the bank, you bound to turn around and when you turn around, I'll whack you."

Meanwhile, my boy was up the roof of the house taking pictures. All of a sudden, he yelled, "Daddy, look down!" There were waves coming up. I swung my net on my back and started home.

My wife was on the porch, she tell, "Throw the net away!"

"No, I think I can beat the wave." So I ran toward the house. Just as I made it to the parlor, a wave came, ripped the floor, and took the kitchen and hallway roofing away. The kitchen broke off from the house; all wrecked into pieces. In no time, the water was bed high, so I tell, "Gee, we better get away from here."

My boy yelled, "Another wave's coming. It looks like it's going to cover the house!"

I says, "Gee, cover the house. We better get back inside. It's better to die in the house. . . . Nobody can find our body if we stay outside."

All of a sudden I hear a crash. "What happened?"

My boy yelled, "We sailing!" Whole house went, cement pillars, too.

The house finally settled down a little over a hundred yards away. The waves started to recede, so I said, "Hey, we better get away." So my wife, my boy and I jumped down into the water. It was a little higher than the chest.

Just then we saw our friend, Takeo. I told him, "Oh, we better run to higher ground."

He said, "Wait, I go get my money and my clothing."

Another wave was coming over the sand dune toward us. Takeo and I were in front. I was holding the baby. My wife and boy was behind me. I tell them, "Climb a tree." So my boy climbed way up high. My wife stood on a branch, a little over one foot above ground because she couldn't climb up. She hang on the tree. Then Takeo climbed another tree about forty feet away.

Then I look at the wave, "Geez, going to cover me. Takeo, hold the baby."

I pushed the baby up to Takeo. I was afraid the wave would throw me off. I can swim, but I cannot save the baby. I held onto the guava tree and was fighting the grass and shrubs, so that it won't knock the tree down.

Then the wave came. It struck me clear. My legs all go off the ground. Only my hand holding the tree.

The wave receded. I looked around. I said, "Takeo, what happened to my wife?"

"Gee, I don't know. I cannot see your wife. I only see your boy."

So I started to swim down. I saw my wife. Her leg was pinned between two trees. I pushed the trees apart as much as I can and told her to pull her leg. All black and blue, but I said, "I know it's sore, but we have to go." Another wave was coming over the sand dune.

We finally made it to higher ground. I looked and saw our house. It went clear inside that stream and wreck up, just like one Lancer box matches. Only the floor was left.

From there, we make our way up to a friend's place. We slept there. The next day, we went to my brother's place in Hilo and stayed there. I look at Hilo. The place was worse hit than Waipio and yet people still get courage to start all over. So I tell my brother, "I'm going back. I'm going to see what I can salvage and start all over again."

You know, just before the waves hit, I brought back $2,000 from the bank for some Chinese taro growers. It was actually their money and I was just like their bank. I was holding their money for them, but that's all gone. And my house is all gone. I lost most of my taro. Some of the taro were still there but cannot be used; the salt water got them.

So I replanted. I drew out money I still had in the bank and went right ahead. But my boy got so disgusted after the tidal wave, he joined the army (laughs).

I don't think my children would like to keep on growing taro. They work at good jobs and everything. I cannot say, "I would like them to

Nelson Chun harvesting water chestnuts in Waipio Valley, 1978. *ESOHP*

take over.'' It's up to them. Taro, if you don't know how, it's hard work. But if you know how, it's easy work. To me, it's just like play. Some fellow, they try pull taro. Back broking and all that kind. To me, I can be pulling taro the whole day, I don't get backache. I still go down to the patches practically every day, sometimes five, six hours, cleaning the banks, weeding, pulling taro.

But I'm getting too old. Cannot work. But if I quit, what am I going to do? I need my exercise. I rather work than just be jogging around and all those stuff. I think working better. You get benefit out of it.

And taro is the only suitable crop for Waipio because the land is all wet. Hard to drain. Of course, there's some land where you can drain 'em and plant another thing, like macadamia nuts and others. But Kona wind bothers macadamia nuts. I have some water chestnuts and lotus planted. The majority of my income is from taro, though.

Waipio means a lot to me. That's my birthplace. I like Waipio. It's peaceful. Of course, I don't know the future too much. And I hope nothing happens.

It all depends on [Bernice Pauahi] Bishop Museum. They own the land. If they going sell out, I don't know who is going to get hold of the land. I wrote, asking them if they would give me a written notice, whether they going sell their land or not within the next five years. They said they cannot tell. They still working on it. They want to sell the whole Waipio, you know. But nobody wants to buy the whole thing. The State like buy a portion of it for parks.

And plenty outside people moving in; they buying land way inside the hillside, those houses. I don't know what kind people. I hope they're all good people. So far no trouble, though. Some of them good workers, too. They pull taro, they clean patch like that. Quite a number of young people going into taro, so I think the future is good. Because not only Hawaiians eat *poi*. Plenty of us eat *poi*.

But production all depend on the climate. If get big floods like that, then going damage a lot. Then taking chance, eh? If it's like these past few years, all right. No big floods so if you plant, you get two crops.

But you never can tell how the taro going come out. If get rot or floods or not. You cannot do anything. That's nature's work.

II
In the City

Eleanor Heavey
MIND, BODY, AND SOUL

Courtesy Alberta Nakaima

The tough, working-class district of Kakaako was home to Eleanor Wilson Heavey. Born on January 18, 1912, to a Hawaiian-Chinese mother and an Australian father, Eleanor had thirteen brothers and sisters, three of whom died during childhood.

The eldest *mo'opuna,* or grandchild, Eleanor spent summers with her maternal grandparents in Kohala. There, she acquired knowledge of Hawaiian culture and a deep appreciation for her Hawaiian heritage. Later in life, she was active in the Hawaiian community as a member of the Hawaiian Civic Club and supporter of the Kahoolawe movement and Aboriginal Lands of Hawaiian Ancestry (ALOHA) organization.

Like many Kakaako women, Eleanor found her first job in the pineapple canneries near home. Only thirteen years old, she packed pineapple on the night shift for sixteen cents an hour until she was discovered to be underage. Still in her teens Eleanor earned three dollars a night playing piano in a dance band.

After another stint at the pineapple cannery, Eleanor became a Navy airplane mechanic during the Second World War and moonlighted as a USO (United Service Organizations) entertainer. From 1943, Eleanor worked for the City's parks and recreation department until her retirement in 1969.

In March 1978, just six months after the interview was conducted, Eleanor Heavey died.

Eleanor's recollections center around Kakaako, a 600–acre waterfront district located next to downtown Honolulu. In the 1920s and 1930s,

Kakaako was a residential community, home to up to 5,000 of the city's working class—laborers, seamen, cannery workers, longshoremen, iron workers, truck drivers, fishermen, county workmen and others. They were housed in tenement-like two-story buildings, duplex cottages, wood-frame camp houses, and in a collection of slapped-together shacks, called Squattersville, near the beach. Eleanor remembers Squattersville as a "Hawaiian paradise" and Queen and Kawaiahao Streets as "where the Portuguese were." While boundaries were far from rigid, Hawaiian, Japanese, and Portuguese families tended to congregate in ethnic "camps," with the less numerous Chinese and Filipinos scattered throughout the district.

A sense of community, however, was felt in sports, community-wide events such as dances and political rallies, and in church and school activities. One of Kakaako's most influential figures during this period was Margaret Waldron, dubbed "Mother Waldron," a Pohukaina School teacher who enlisted "bad boys" and downtown businessmen alike in her efforts to provide educational and recreational opportunities for the community's young people.

The Kakaako of residences and small businesses described by Eleanor has given way in the aftermath of post-World War II zoning changes to a Kakaako of warehouses, automotive repair shops and other service and light industries.

Eleanor's two interview sessions were part of a 1978 project entitled, "Remembering Kakaako: 1910–1950." The interviewer was Perry Nakayama, then a recent University of Hawaii graduate. "Eleanor Heavey was," Perry says, "the kind of 'auntie' that kept you in line as you grew up." He remembers Eleanor as an animated speaker, very relaxed, and not at all intimidated by the tape recorder. The first interview session took place under the trees in Pine Grove, Waimanalo. The sounds of passing cars and the screeching of parrots overhead could be heard in the background. A subsequent session was held at the Moiliili Community Center, where Eleanor had just finished teaching a ukulele class for senior citizens. In spite of poor health, she was in good spirits.

Eleanor's interview was especially candid and imbued with feeling. Her use of language was unique, her phrasing melodic and rhythmic. Special pains were taken to retain those qualities in this narrative.

"It's all in my storehouse, the beautiful things that have happened. You talk about tragic, there's been so little, and far between. I feel sorry for kids today. Every hardship is the end of the world. But the hardship that you get is a building up of your body, mind, and spirit for future things. If we do not get a little bit of starvation, little bit of joblessness, little bit of hardship, what the hell good are we as people? This is not a smooth-walking world made out of velvet to walk on softly. It is a rough road. But the beauty about walking on this road is that, there's going to be some smooth asphalt.''

A Pretty Good Bringing Up

ELEANOR ELIZABETH NAHIAPO, that's my Hawaiian name.

My father was a seaman. He worked on a ship all his life. Mama came from Kohala. She was born in Niulii as Namahana KooMahuka. My mother's father came from Punaluu. He's known as KooMahuka, the famous Mahuka family. They were not chiefs but overseers for the chiefs. They held important positions. So Mama was educated in Sacred Heart Convent on Fort Street. I had to tell you about my mother and father because they had an interesting life.

My mother was raised in Kohala, a regular country jack. I mean, people from Kohala, they don't know too much about city people and city life, and live a typical country life. They catch their own fish, and know how and where to get their *limu,* or seaweed. They don't depend on stores. Mama had three sisters, herself made four. They were sent to Honolulu to be educated. So all of them had up to eighth-grade education, which was considered very good those days. One of my aunties went to Normal School to receive her teaching degree. But Mama married.

Mama met my father, Harry Wilson, who was from Australia. My father was on a ship and didn't want to go back to Australia, so he got off in Kakaako. He spoke with a heavy English accent, and the ''nickel and dime'' boys, who dived for coins tossed from passenger ships, thought he was really a novelty to have around in Kakaako. A kid that spoke with a strange language. It sounded like *haole,* but it wasn't really *haole.* He also became a ''nickel and dime'' diver. And he met my mother, and they got married.

Papa was always on a ship—*Cleveland, Lurline,* all of these ships that carried cargo back and forth to the Orient, to Alaska. My aunties got married to men from the ships because my father brought these men home. They were all nice-looking men, so my aunties got married to them. They got land jobs and, later, jobs with the State and the City. But Papa liked going to sea.

That's why we lived in Kakaako. It was close to the ocean, just a stone's throw to Pier 2, Pier 11, Pier 12, and all the piers. It's just a walking distance. So you find that even the Seamen Hospital and the Seamen Homes was right in Kakaako, too. When seamen got off ship and didn't have any place to go, that's their home. You know, they would work maybe six, eight months in a year, come back on land till their money ran out, and then went on ship again.

So, that was the kind of life my father had. And we grew up used to it, see. We see our father and all of a sudden we don't see him for eight months, sometimes to a year. When he came in, there was gifts galore from wherever—whatever country he went to. And we always like when he went to Japan and China, because then he would come home with lot of toys and exciting things that other kids in the neighborhood did not have.

You know, pearls, my father used to bring 'em home. Each of us had a pearl. But we knew nothing of its value. I wish my father would have told us, "This is from the oysters and it's very valuable." But he just gave it to us as a gift, and it was just like toys that he brought along, too. So pretty soon we used it for hopscotch. You think about how foolish we were, and Mama never stopped us. She kept her pearl necklaces and little trinkets that my father brought, but she let us kids do what we wanted with ours. And they were genuine pearls that Papa brought back, see. In Japan and China, things were so cheap that American money can buy about anything. It was exciting when he came back from the Orient.

That is a small part of my father and mother's life when they first met. And every year my mother would have a baby; a baby, every year.

Mama always had a midwife for her children. My father handled the hot water and whatever the midwife needed. All of us kids was put in one room, and we waited till we can hear the baby cry.

The Portuguese women were the midwives. Very clean. This was their job, when they left Portugal. And it was passed down from one daughter to another daughter. So, most of the midwives that I can remember were Portuguese. I never saw any Hawaiian midwives, I never saw any Japanese.

People didn't have big money, so whatever the midwife was getting—I think it was ten dollars—that was good money. See, and she might have maybe three, four cases. Once the baby is born, the midwife comes in, she teaches how to take care of the *piko,* "navel." And how to bathe, how to oil the child up; so she worked sometimes a week, or two weeks, after the child is born.

I was the number one, first-born, in the family. You know, when I sit back and think, we had a pretty good home, and my father was a good supporter. My father and mother had their problems, but overall, we had a pretty good bringing-up.

We had plenty kids—thirteen. That was one of the problems. Sometime wasn't enough room for all of the kids. You study or you want to do something, you've got kids crawling all over you.

By the time I was around fifteen, sixteen, the last one was born. Of course, Mama lost two boys at two, three years old from the flu epidemic. At that time we were in Palama. Then we moved back into Kakaako and lost one girl from that same illness. So that brought the family down to ten.

Those days, pneumonia, people died. And the flu. To us today, it's nothing. One year when they had the flu epidemic, I was in the second grade, I believe. People dropped, died. The only protection we had, so we thought, was to have this bag of camphor on your neck! So you smell it every time in school and when you playing. When you think about it today, that camphor bag is nothing! Maybe psychologically, it saved a lot of us, but the camphor has no power whatsoever to kill the virus. We didn't know it at that time. You get pneumonia, you die. You get the flu, you died.

You know, there was a funny feeling among Kakaako people. The doctors at Queen's Hospital was all white people. And Hawaiians say that if you're going to Queen's Hospital, you're sure to come out feet first. Sure, there were some good doctors there. I remember a Dr. McDonald. He always encouraged Hawaiians and the people of Kakaako. And, Dr. Hayes was another old one. Hawaiians went to him because he was married to a Hawaiian woman. But, anybody else, they didn't trust.

Number one, the Hawaiians didn't trust the white man. The white men brought nothing for the Hawaiians to trust. You understand. They were very dishonest. They exploited, they lied. Now, my *tūtū* says the word *haole, ha* means "breath," *ole* means "breath with nothing." You're a lie, it's nothing to that breath. I don't want to harp on that. Anyway, they stayed away from the hospital.

There were times when they should have had doctors, and they didn't have, so they died, I guess, from lack of attention. But the Hawaiians had their herbs, so they took quite a lot of that to stay away from the hospital.

Every Hawaiian in the neighborhood had some knowledge of what was good. *Pōpolo* [a weed with black berries] was good for your colds and congested chest. You take that. And the *'uha-loa,* oh, my mother used to go get us to go pick up this *'uha-loa.* It's a Hawaiian herb. Now, it's only a small plant, but you try dig 'em out. You might as well need a bomb or dynamite to blow the thing out. I had the job of digging it out, and how I hated it. Afterwards, I tell my mother, "I had to stay there, and I dug, and I dug, and I dug, and I dug, and you'd ask me to strip the bark and I did. Now, to kill this illness, I have to chew it up." I says, "No, Mama. I'll stay with the disease."

You Divided Your Beliefs

There was *kahuna*s in Kakaako, too. *Kahuna* was a frightening word. You didn't use it freely in the household. You didn't say, "Eh, so-and-so is *kahuna,*" or "Let's go see the *kahuna,*" just like you would say, "Let's go see a doctor" today. You have the good *kahuna,* you have the bad *kahuna.* Then again, you had Christians and non-Christians. So you divided your beliefs.

I was brought up a Christian and always wondered, "How come these people go to *kahuna*s when they have Christ to turn to?" Well, it was easy for me to say that, but we didn't know how to use Christ those days, either. Unless you know how to use Christ, you will not get the *mana,* the power to heal, the power to receive. You understand? But when the Hawaiians were sick, and they prayed and didn't get any relief, it was understood: "I want life. Now I love this man Christ. But I'm not getting any relief." So they ran to whom? To the *mana* of the pagan, if you want to say that. Only if the illness does not go away after they've taken all kinds of herbs and after they've even had a white man doctor, and it doesn't go away, this is when they'll go to a *kahuna.* For what? To *ho'oponopono.*

"Is this disease from something I have done? Or is this disease caused by a curse that an ordinary doctor or ordinary herbs cannot take away?" So when you go to *ho'oponopono,* the *kahuna* can take this word or this curse off. And if you have wronged someone, then you are to apologize to your wife, to your children first, and then later to whoever is around you—your neighbor, storekeepers, or whatever. And so this is the only purpose for *kahuna* down in Kakaako. By the time I left Kakaako in 1938, not too much of the word *kahuna* was heard.

In my younger life, right up to the age of thirteen, I think, they used to have a fireball that flew over the ocean and landed anywhere close to our house. That is not a falling star, like most of the white men would talk about. It is low and has a long tail and fiery ball in the front. That fireball brings death from whoever had sent this.

These fireballs would come from Molokai and Kauai. Lanai was supposed to have some, but the most powerful came from Molokai and Kauai. Now, what I'm telling you are only the stories that I got from the Hawaiian people there. I did no research. Only from their mouths, I heard that Molokai and Kauai were the two islands that carried evil *kahunas*. You wanted death, this is the two islands you went to.

I know the Japanese didn't know too much about this fireball, Chinese didn't know too much about it, but the Hawaiians would curse it to kill the power. They know that it is being sent for no good, so they curse it. " *'Ai kūkae 'oe* (Eat shit)! *Eia* (Here's yours)! *Pilau maoli no 'oe* (You're so rotten)!" This is the way they throw their words. " *'Auhea 'oe hele ana* (Where do you think you're going)? *Auwē* (Oh)! *'Ai kanaka 'oe* (You're a killer)!" This is to kill the curse, to kill the power. If somebody passed away, then the people know that their words didn't hold any power.

Everyone Is Related to You

Then when somebody died, everybody went to the undertaking parlor. Now, the Hawaiians just love undertaking parlors! They love to go to visit all the dead people. So they would go in there and *kūō*. *Kūō* means "to cry." Now, country people is used to this. "*E, kūō, kūō kēia keiki hana ku'u ponopono o kēia hoaloha* (Yeah, they would wail and cry about this child who worked for my welfare, about this friend). . . ." Then, how he was born, where he was born, and all that. If I had any sense those days, if I wanted to know about certain people, all you do is listen to all this *kūō* and chanting. Actually, they telling you the genealogy of this person, see. But I never cared to go because you would hear the wailing. No forget, I was brought up in the city.

Anyway, Mama used to drag me all the time, being the oldest. She would say, "*A kēia kou ko 'ohana* (And this is your relative)." I look, and don't even see how this person is related to me. Mama had a mind of a walking genealogy. She knew just where you came from, who, and what. She was just wonderful, when it came to that. My mother says, "This is your cousin. This is your auntie, this is uncle." Everyone is related to you. And till today, you meet all of your relatives, all of your friends, people that you've never seen long time, where? At the undertaking.

Let me tell you of this experience I had. Old man died in a house.

They call several men to come give the person a bath. Then, we call it Hawaiian salt—later, this rock salts were imported, but we originally got our own salt from our own land. So they would stuff the *'ōkole* with salt. They worked it in with *tī* leaves. Underneath the armpit, they would cut and stuff the salt. This is the way they embalmed. You know how they cut the pig up and put salt inside. Was very much like that. And the body could stay for three, four days. The better the job is, the longer the body would stay.

Now, I remember, they did have a box, which came from the undertaking parlor, which was lined with velvet. You know how they have this embroidered velvet or satin? All embroidered with flowers and stuff. You no see me wear those kind of clothing. You no see me buy furniture covering with that kind. Yeah. Mentally, I think of this one coffin, when I was a little child.

So, they make me sit down and fan this body from the flies. Well, the fan fell into the coffin, and I reached down to pick it up. I touched the dead person's face, thinking it was warm. You're used to warm people, but it's cold as ice, and stiff, and hard. Till today I have never been able to kiss a dead person. Be it my father, my mother, my sisters. So, all my affection is shown when they're alive. To caress, to hold, to hug, to kiss. Once they're gone, all the rest of the family can go kiss. But I've already done mine.

Gorgeous Childhood Summers

The experience I started to tell you about embalming the body, that was held in Kohala. See, I spent my childhood days during the summer with my *tūtū* in Kohala. I was queen when I go over there. My grandfather work daytime at the plantation. Seventy-five cents a day. This money was used for little grocery things and for me, the oldest *mo'opuna*, to come to Kohala during the summer.

I'm very thankful for those summers, 'cause this is where I got most of my Hawaiiana spirit. In the city, there's not too much. But when you go to the country, when there's no more running water, when your toilet is an earth-dug toilet, where your fish is coming from the ocean and from the stream, where you get your taro from the taro patches —this is typical country.

In the country, they all spoke Hawaiian, and I didn't. They warble off, look at me, and bump me because I'm a foreigner. You go to the outer islands those days, those country kids take you for one foreigner.

Hawaiian child, Kohala, Hawaii, 1908. *Courtesy Ray Jerome Baker Collection, Bishop Museum*

On the islands, the Japanese spoke Hawaiian, the Chinese spoke Hawaiian, the *haole*s spoke Hawaiian. You one Hawaiian no can speak Hawaiian, you foreigner. I don't belong there. They hit me, and I going look for my *tūtū* for tell 'em about what the kids were doing.

And, I remember those days in Kohala, they were all Christians. There was church services so Sunday, you get dressed. My grandfather would hold his shoes in his hand; my grandmother hold my shoes in her hand, put me on a horse. Just because I came from the city didn't mean I like shoes. And you're all dressed up with white pique, and ribbon on the hair and hat. You travel for miles. Might take you an hour on horseback to get to the church. When you get there, all the Hawaiians with their *lau hala* hat, with their little high-neck dresses, and same thing, holding the shoes in the hand. As soon as the bell start ringing, they put on the shoes, walk inside the church.

Then when the church is over, get on the horse again. The *poi,* the fish, they put 'em on the side of the horse. Go down to the beach.

Hali'i, or spread, all these things down on the table, or on the ground; everybody comes over and share the potluck. They got their Hawaiian brew. They drink up, sing up, and eat up. And I'm happy with them. This gorgeous childhood summers that I had with my *tūtū.*

The Little Pleasant Memories That Made Kakaako

But Kakaako was my home. I'm happy with the Kakaako people. That's why I say, it was a blessing to live among Kakaako people. To me, I say, "God meant this to be like this for me. If He meant it different, I would have been raised up in the country with my grandfolks. But He didn't want me. This was not in the planning."

In Kakaako, we had a two-story house, three bedrooms upstairs. We were fortunate. We didn't have to pay too much for a carpenter. My *tūtū,* my grandfather KooMahuka, did all of the building. My father is a painter, also. So he painted it. Four, five years it'd be red, and the next four or five years, it would be white. The next four or five years would be brown. Then come back to red again.

My mother was a good *lau hala* weaver. Upstairs is always covered with *lau hala.* For sleeping purposes, we have two, three big *lau hala* mats. We would flop that in this extra room. That room was about fifteen by fifteen feet. Those days, bedrooms and parlors was very large compared to what it is today. And that was what we used when we had guests, kids, grownups. We didn't have TV. But we had so much fun just lying around talking story and listening to the old folks.

Actually, the whole downstairs was, I would say, maybe forty by forty feet. That's downstairs alone. You have your bathroom, and your toilet. Then, the rest of the place there is wide open. It was not divided.

Your kitchen was right there, downstairs—your stove, your sink. We had oil stove. I think everybody in that neighborhood had kerosene stove. You buy a whole gallon for ten, fifteen cents. And that kerosene would last for about a whole week and a half. That's cheaper than electricity and gas. The gallon is attached to the stove. Then you lift up a gadget, and you take out your gallon, you go to the store, fill it up, bring it back again.

And the icebox, that was a diller. Oh, I'm telling you. You wait for the iceman to bring the ice. Twenty-five pound, and you lift up the blasted thing, put 'em inside this so-called icebox. Then by the end of the day, the ice is all melted and your food is all spoiled.

Now, my father was a good cook, and he loved to eat bird, dove. No forget I'm Hawaiian. Coming from a nation or group of people, these are the things they don't eat. But I learned to eat doves, I learned to eat pigeon, and I learned to eat rabbit.

Papa loved to cook stew meat, lamb, curry, any kind, because he brought home the menus from the different parts of the world. And he used me for guinea pig to try it out because he loved my mother so dearly and never wanted to lay anything before my mother that was not so *ono*. And me, I love food. You cook 'em, I never tell you it's junk. How can I tell you it's junk when I don't know how to cook? I eat it. I say, "It's good, Papa."

He's the chief cook in our household. He knows what he's doing. We were never ashamed to invite friends over if he did the cooking.

When it was during the depression, Papa used to go down to work for the City and County as a laborer. Every man worked, but fifteen days on, fifteen days off. So, my father, during the fifteen days that he was off, would go down to catch squid. Now remember, he's not a Hawaiian, but he's been around Hawaiian boys. He knows how to use a glass box to catch squid. So he would catch sometime ten, fifteen squid, bring it home. And him and I would sit down and we'd pound it to get it soft. Put Hawaiian salt in a big pan. You grab each squid, and you pound it till it all gets curly and that slime all gets up, and you rinse it. Because one big squid can feed a big family, my father would cook one, dry the rest. That would be food for the kids, see. There was no such thing as starving if you go look.

Then my mama would go with him. You know where is Squattersville? That was a place near the beach where squatters, mostly Hawaiian, lived. That was the Hawaiian paradise. You had squid, you had *'ōpae*, "shrimp," you had *wana* and *hāwa'e*, "sea urchin." You had anything you wanted that was Hawaiian in there. Mama would go get *limu*. Or go get the *wana* or *'ina*, the baby sea urchin. Come home, my father would cook what he's supposed to cook. My mother would fix the raw stuff and the *poi*. If no more *poi*, get the rice done. Most of the time there was *poi* because of Mama.

My mother was typical Hawaiian. It was either raw fish, *poi*, or dried shrimp. If it was stew meat, you won't find potatoes, you won't find onions in there, you won't find no vegetables, 'cause Mama only wanted her meat with gravy. That's all. That's it. No more potatoes, no more nothing. She said she didn't want all the junks inside.

Mama wasn't an extravagant person. There were many times when we had only one dollar left in the house. And when the kids were all on the dining table, she would put that dollar right down and say, "This is all we got till your father gets back. Hopefully by this week." This sort of thing does not hurt a household; you share the gladness, and the happiness, as well as the hardship.

Mama always bought a whole bag of flour and a whole bag of rice. Have *poi* too, but if no more money, you got to fall on those two things. We didn't have plenty of meat with our rice, but she would pick up maybe dried shrimp with onions and stretch it. This is a good mother. This is a good father who can stretch your food till the bulk of the money comes in. Not say, "Oh, we don't have this. We don't have that." So, I've learned through that, you know.

When things get so rough, my mother would make a dish—you'd laugh, I tell you—which we weren't used to seeing too often, thank God. She would soak the flour, put a little baking powder—very little baking powder—and she would mix this dough-like stuff. And she would dump these little balls of flour, baking powder, little salt, little sugar in this hot water, and boil it. Then she'd throw this condensed milk inside and make it sweet, you know.

And us kids come home from school, she says, "Well, your lunch is right there. That's supper, too."

"What is it?"

"Hawaiian doughnuts."

"Hawaiian doughnuts!"

Gee whiz! Hard as a rock. No more meat, no more fish, no more nothing with it so you fix yourself a bowl of that. You start off with one first. And if you still hungry, then you go get another. What you call that now? *Pa'i a'i*. Hawaiians call it *Pa'i a'i* because it's not enough baking powder.

For us, seven o'clock in the morning would be breakfast, because everybody go to school. Got to leave the house by eight o'clock. Breakfast, most times we didn't have any big meals. Just grab something. Grab, sit down and fix tea, fix coffee, fix milk chocolate.

Lunch, sometimes we had money, sometimes we didn't have money. That was kind of rough on that part. We never had too much. If there was any bread, or butter, or jelly, or anything, then we would take that. Because all of us were going to school, see. There isn't enough money, even though the lunches were cheap. Five cents and ten cents.

And during my time, the Chinese used to come around to sell pork cakes. You know, the *mea'ono-pua'a* man. See, the word *manapua* is cut short for *mea'ono-pua'a*. See, *mea* means "things." *Ono* means "good things." And *pua'a* means "pork." So as the word went along, nobody like use *mea'ono-pua'a*. They go "*Mana-, mana-, manapua.*" And that's wrong. *Mea'ono-pua'a* is the right word. Yeah. So he would come around nearly every day. Sometimes they go to where the workingmen is, and their wares are all gone. So they go home, and then they get a refill. Then they come back again to another section.

Then we hear him, "*Manapua! Pepeiao! 'Ōkole!*"

"Mama, the *manapua* man." Exciting. See, they'd call out their wares throughout the neighborhood.

And five cents, you can get *manapua.* You can get *pepeiao* and *'ōkole.* Three for five cents. So, that was plenty for lunch. And then, he would come certain days with ice cream. Ice cream cone. All by hand grinding. You seen the kind of homemade ice cream. So wherever he stop, grind, and delicious! Oh! And that's two for five cents.

See, and that was good money to the people. The Japanese and Chinese were terrific merchants. Because back home, this is what they did for a living. You understand. Talk about imagination and determination, this is one thing I give them credit for—this beautiful initiative. There isn't a hell of a lot of money in their country. So they go, according to America's ways.

And there was a Japanese candy man. He's got a big, big pan. About I'd say, two by three feet. It's made out of tin. And his candy is hard candy. What do you call the kind you stretch? Taffy. You have never tasted *ono* taffy like his. Today's candy makers stingy, so they leave out all the good ingredients that make good candy. Those days, they know how to make candy. Pink ones, white ones, yellow ones. And he get the hammer, and he crack it with his little hammer right there. All broke into pieces. Big package for five cents. I can taste it now. Man, and nice and neat. He always wore a white jacket, a white hat. And he would walk. "Candy! Candy! Candy!" We'd run. "The candy man, the candy man! Five cents."

And my grandmother, she was a saver of money. Most Hawaiians were not extravagant. To have a good time, they didn't know what the hell to do with money. So, they smoke. They grew their own tobacco. Then, when the tobacco leaf was ready, they would roast it on the charcoal. They would crush it in a little cigar box called *pahu-puhi paka.* That means a box for her smoke. But in that box, it would be so filled with tobacco. You put your finger in and you would find nickels, and you keep searching. What a beautiful game we used to have.

I said, "*Tūtū,* I want five cents."

"*No ke ana* (What for)?"

I tell, "The candy man. *Ke kanakē.*" I didn't know how to talk Hawaiian too much. "The *kanakē, kanakē* man."

" '*Ae, hele ki'i i loko ka pahu-puhi paka* (Yes, go get it inside the tobacco box)."

I put my hand inside, I find one five cents, I find one dime.

"*Tūtū,* I can have the dime?"

" '*Ae* (Yes)."

I go buy two package and come back. She and I sit down and eat candy. Those are the little pleasant memories that made Kakaako. The candy man, the *mea'ono-pua'a* man. The *saimin* lady.

Oh, yeah. Was a *saimin* noodle soup lady that in the evening, when the working people would come home, she had one of these red wagons pulled by hand. Those wagons came from Japan. Two big wheels, little lattice-work. In the inside of it would be two big pots of hot water. There'd be charcoal underneath burning to keep it hot. On the side of this little wagon, she would have her eggs all chopped up, meat, *shōyu,* whatever ingredients she needed was right there.

From the time she entered into our lane, the smell of the soup broth tells you the *saimin* lady is at the entrance, now get your money ready. Ten cents for one big *saimin* bowl. So you divide your ten cents bowl with another kid. Half and a half. Fifty cents would feed this big family of ten for *saimin.* Then you have the barbecue stick. Five cents, one. With three meats on top. The smell would be so strong, and so nice that you cannot let the *saimin* lady pass. You got to go look for ten cents! Even if meant tomorrow you going starve, you look for that ten cents.

"The *saimin* lady, Mama. The *saimin* lady."

"Okay, I hid fifty cents underneath the rug. Go look for it."

Hoo, when she says that, it opens up a big door.

See, how long you have these people coming in. It is that which makes Kakaako, which makes living in Hawaii.

But they gradually disappeared. The *manapua* man still came by, but his prices went up. Everything else went up just before World War II. The *saimin* lady got a house with a nice yard in Kakaako and she build a stand. So everybody went over to her stand, and she made such terrific *saimin.* Those days, we were drinking beer, and they had nightclubs right around our place. So as soon as the nightclub close, we'd go over there and call out, "Mama-*san,*" and she'd open up, and we'd have *saimin* and barbecue meat.

And then, during the weekend, the Portuguese would bake extra bread. Both the white bread and sweet bread. This is why I'm spoiled having been brought up eating that kind of food, good Japanese food, good Chinese food, good Portuguese food. Their homemade bread, if they charge me five dollars for one loaf, I'll buy that.

Now, the Portuguese, who owned their property, you see them with a oven in the back. It's made out of bricks. They'd bake during the weekend. And their yeast was made out of potato. They let it ferment, and they mix that yeast with their bread, you know. You can smell it for miles, their bread.

They sold it, twenty-five cents a loaf. So they, too, earned a little money. Their sweet bread was little bit more. They would put it in a basket. The Portuguese women would put it on their head, and they would walk down the road. We knew already. This is the day they're selling bread.

"Mary, you have bread?"

"Yeah."

"Give us two."

Clean-faced Kids

In Kakaako, we had Portuguese that occupied Queen Street, Kawaiahao Street. That's where the majority of the Portuguese were. And the Catholic church—most of the Portuguese are Catholic—was on Kamani Street, which is just an off-street from Queen and Kawaiahao. So, that was the only Catholic church we have there, known as St. Agnes. We were Catholics at the time. My mother graduated from Sacred Heart Convent, so she was Catholic-trained. And all her kids that she born and raised were baptized in Catholic church, until later on in years when my mother started to seek for more knowledge of the Lord. She left the Catholic Church, which was considered a mortal sin. Well, the Portuguese were one of the strongest Catholic members in Kakaako. And handful of Hawaiians. Those days, you hardly see any Japanese in the Catholic church. And you hardly saw any Chinese. You only saw Portuguese and Hawaiian.

Although we went Catholic church, we didn't dig all that stuff, you know. From Monday to Sunday, I believe that the Portuguese kids were really kids that you'd like to give 'em a backhand. We go to catechism, and they would be over there, bringing their goodies to eat, and showing it off to the other kids. We not supposed to do this in catechism. But they would do it, these things that annoyed you.

Once a year, on this particular day, they going to have this great big feast day, the Holy Ghost Festival. The statue of Jesus is carried on a

Holy Ghost festival in Kakaako, c. 1920s. *Courtesy Gloria Felix*

platform. Then all these kids would have little wings, little halos, you know, all dressed in white. And by golly, parents go out of their way to make all these outfits for these cute little angels that are going to walk on the street.

All us *kanaka* kids would be standing on the side of the road, watching.

"Look at that. Look at that."

"Hoo, he's so holy. Look at him. He looks so holy today."

Marching in the street. No smile on the face, carrying this statue on the shoulders, and the band would be playing, *pa-pa-shukoom-pong, pa-pa-shukoom-pong, pa-pa-shukoom-pong-pong-pong!* as-they-march-on-the-road-so-sweet. Aw, every year. They'd march from the Catholic church on down to the place they call the Holy Ghost ground. And the statue is taken into this little chapel, and the little angels are all around.

Oh, the parade would be about half a mile maybe. With St. Theresa's Society, Portuguese men, and the catechism kids. We go catechism, but we don't get in the parade. Only this clean-faced kids would be marching down the road. Ah, us kids were monsters. That's because we didn't care for them. And I suppose they didn't care for us.

This is a personal opinion—I don't know if the rest of the kids felt the same way towards the Portuguese kids. Although I didn't care for them, I didn't really hate them. I didn't like the way they talk. Their English was very, very poor. They emphasize when they speak on the "bins" and the "wases." "Eh, where you going? What you doing? You know what I bin doing?" That kind of a talk. I just despised it. And you couldn't change it. That's the way they were.

And I think little things like this. We were in the sixth grade. But after sixth-grade graduation, these Portuguese girls would be getting married already. They were burly, big women. See, I graduated when I was fourteen years old. So that made the difference, too. Most of the girls graduated at sixteen. So they got married. There was something that I didn't care about Portuguese.

At That Time, To Learn Was Very Important

Don't forget I went to Kakaako Sunday School, remember. They had all color crayons. These seem to be very unimportant now, but those days, you couldn't get crayons, like how you do now. So at that time, to learn was very important. You were eager as an individual. You learn to make use of all the color crayons that they have because you don't have at home. And if you can swipe one or two without being so sinful, you'd swipe one or two.

Then, too, my mother graduated from Sacred Heart Convent. Although it's only eighth grade, that was quite a big schooling for those kids those days. So the household had quite a lot of reading material. My grandfather subscribed for the *Kū'oko'a,* and he would read out loud in his Hawaiian, see. He'd sit down over there and he'd *ka mea, ka mea, kūlolou* (this and that, this and that, etc.). I would sit there and look at my *tūtū.* He wouldn't be reading to me, he'd be reading to himself. Then I would catch on to all the different things he was saying. He was an educated man, too. He went to Lahainaluna School on Maui.

Me, I learned how to read when I was in the first grade. That's why I can't understand why kids today cannot read, even though they graduate from high school. And I feel sorry. See, I think at that time, reading was very important. I was alway curious about what was in the newspaper, the pictures and all of that. Magazines was beginning to come out. If you don't know how to read, you don't know what it's all about.

At Pohukaina School, I got a lot of loving attention from the *hapa-haole,* or part-white and part-Hawaiian teachers. Nearly everyone was *hapa-haole.* The Whittle family, Mrs. Wilson, a Mrs. Johnson, Mrs. Brede, and, of course, Mrs. Waldron—everyone called her Mother Waldron. And we used to get this math teacher. Aw, shucks. He was a bachelor, see. So all the Hawaiian girls stupid in math, you know. And this darn teacher used to look at all our legs. Hey, this bachelor, he must be hungry for woman or something. So, those who wanted to get good marks, all they did was put the legs outside. He go up and down, he look. He no call us. So the same kind of mischievousness was going on those days as it does today.

But not too much of play hookey. I think most time the kids, if they stayed home, was because they didn't have lunch money. We had truant officers that went to check what happened to them. And most time it was you don't want to go school with no more lunch, eh?

Everyone was in the same boat. Sometime would be crackers. We bought crackers by the big can. No more butter. So what we do, we get the cracker, and we put sugar. Just get it damp enough so that the sugar would act like jelly, you know. And then my neighbor, Japanese, would carry one small little can, and they would have *ume,* or "pickled plum," inside, and *daikon,* "radish," and little fish.

It was later on in life, when our neighbor—we were still friends—says, "You know, I used to like eat your cracker!"

And I says, "I look at you eating your *ume,* and I like your *ume.*"

He said, "Why didn't you ask me?"

I said, "You know, those days, we don't ask, eh."

And neither do we steal, neither do we take somebody else's lunch. There was quite a lot of respect with people's things in those days.

I don't know where she got her money, but Mother Waldron put some money up for free lunches for certain kids. That was kind of nice. We didn't have a cafeteria really, so where she was getting her free lunches, I don't know. But the words, "underprivileged and poor," wasn't too much thrown to us, you know. And I kind of like that. It was later on in years, when I hear them all talking about "underprivilege." And before you know it, well, the kids are smart. Says, "Oh, if I'm poor, I can get this free." Where in my time, we didn't want that because we had too much pride to go to the welfare.

We'd Feel For One Another

Mother Waldron was also in charge of lot of activities in Kakaako. She was well known with American Factors, and C. Brewer and Company, all those big shots, where she would get the kind of equipments that the government couldn't afford. Where other districts didn't have it, we had it because she went out to get those stuff. Yeah, she was pretty *akamai,* "smart," and forceful. Very forceful person.

You've gone to visit Pohukaina School, yeah? Right in front, that whole area was Atkinson Park. Was a very interesting park. We had swings, sliding boards, nearly all the equipment of recreation now. And we had a little shack that Mother Waldron took care of. All our equipment, baseball, volleyball, all the balls were inside. When we want to borrow it, we go see Mother Waldron.

Then, all along by the incinerator, that was called Squattersville. And Squattersville had a stone wall, and it was called "Stone Wall." The waves over there were so beautiful—too beautiful for me to leave alone. Oh, I used to love the ocean!

My mother said, "I want you home here right after school."

"Yes, Mama, yes, Mama."

But my bathing suit already under the *kiawe,* or "algaroba," tree. Never see me till dark. That's why I always had dirty lickings. I'm supposed to be home at 5:30, 6:30, I'm not. I'm down at the beach.

This kid right next to me, one of the Huihui boys, had one of those heavy surfboards. Anytime you wanted to ride on it, you had to help carry that board down the beach. And boy, I was always willing to help. Only time I can ride it is when the other kids were tired.

And sometime I get the board, sometime I don't. And you sit there, and you be patient to wait till your turn comes. Oh, when you catch the waves, and you just ride, and you ride, and you ride, and you come in, your body is sore. By the time you come in, well, it's dark. I know it's *pau* suppertime. I going get licking. All of us *hāpai* the board, bring the board. And here I am, walking with this big board, carrying with these kids. The guy who owned the board, he's a big cheese, ah.

We also dive at Stone Wall. We stick a plank out in the stone wall and learn how to dive over there. It's so much more fun to dive in the ocean than it is to dive in the pool. You learn how to swan dive or all that kind of different dives. Half the time, no more coach. You just going to learn on your own and then see what you turn out.

And I also played baseball. I was a catcher. My sister Hannah was in the star category. I was never a star. We picked up a whole bunch of star players. Yeah, we had some pretty first top people.

One of the Chinese girls was first baseman. A few Chinese came in. They had to do something. They young people, too, eh. Even though the father and mother didn't want 'em to hang around Hawaiians. But youth, you cannot keep youth in a prison. They've got to find youth for company. This Chinese friend I'm talking about almost married a half-white boy. But the father and mother squashed that romance. So, to please them, she married a Chinese. Then the second sister ran away and got married to a Portuguese boy. Then that left only one brother. And he, in turn, to please the father and mother, got married to a Chinese.

More so, the Japanese didn't want their kids to hang around any other nationality but their own. Even that kind of a marriage, where they brought the bride or the bridegroom from Japan, was still going on. And some of my schoolmates had gotten mixed up in that kind of a stuff and then had to get a divorce 'cause they couldn't stand it. I mean, was so unfair, you know. If you came from that kind of a tradition, if you were in Japan, you would accept it. But here we are in another country. It gave us some freedom to pick up on our own love.

Then my Japanese friend later told me, "You know, Eleanor," she says, "to have a stranger take you to bed." And we didn't know anything about sex. In my case, I was sixteen, seventeen, and I was still thinking that the kids came from one *puka*, "hole," on a shelf. As many kids as we had in our household. So sex was not a free subject. And this was very unfair to young people to have a stranger from Japan come and take them to bed.

This came from my friend that we went to school together, graduated together. She says, "Oh, you folks are lucky. At least you folks had your choice of picking up your own man." She says, "And here I am. They had planned for this wedding, and I get this guy, and all the Japanese bring out all the headgears, all the flour powder on the face."

When I saw her, I said, "That cannot be her." But yet it was.

Then those who wanted to marry their own choice, they ran away. See, in McKinley High School, they picked their own girls and they picked up their own husbands. But if the family liked it, was fine.

This one boy was kind of sweet on me, and he was Portuguese to begin with. And Mama didn't know. He says, "Come on, Eleanor, let's go to the show," and I would go. And he was such a gentleman. He was one of the smart Portuguese. Never forgot him. So, he took me to the Princess Theater. My mother heard about it, and she said I was a wicked girl to go with him. Those days, if the mothers didn't like you, they put you in the girl's training school. My mother thought it was best for me to go to girl's training school. Right here in Moiliili. All the bad girls were inside there. But there wasn't too many bad girls. And poor thing, the kids those days everything was sinful.

You see, that sort of thing was going on in our neighborhood. So there was good and bad. And we'd feel for one another. Just like the youth is today. They feel for one another.

Scolley's Moonlight Six

See, the parents would be awfully strict. But where everything happened was at the dances. Oh, that was just the place for romancing. You had your boyfriend, you'd meet him there.

So the mother would say, "You go to the dance, you make sure you home by 11:30."

So all you hear, "Yes, Mama, yes, Mama. I'll be home at 11:30."

Armory Hall, Palama Settlement, that's about the only places that was famous for dancing Friday and Saturday night. Oh, and Kewalo Club in the immediate district of Kakaako. It's a small clubhouse. As a matter of fact, it was a barn to store grain. Then it was later converted into a boxing arena.

Whether it was a church, whether it was a society, they sponsored dances and hired their own orchestra.

My uncle had an orchestra. He played his saxophone but studied his music from a pianola. He would buy the songs on a roller and put it in the pianola. And he would learn. After all the musicians would go home after rehearsal, he would pump. Make it slow, and he'd watch the different movements on the piano. Then he would copy. He would get all the changes from the piano. I'd watch him. What a smart man. So this is going on for about a year or two, when he's got his orchestra, and I'm so proud. See, while the orchestra was singing and playing, I would sit there and catch on all their songs.

So one day I come from school, and here's a piano inside our house. I am the most joyful person in the whole world!

So I says, "Mama, how come this piano came in ?"

"Well, your uncle couldn't make the payments."

"And then what happened?"

"So I agreed on taking the piano over, and your father says he'll pay for the piano."

Oh, how nice. How marvelous. How beautiful! So I learned how to play. I watch Uncle learning how to play the piano through rolling and slowing it down. That's how I learned. I did the same as he did. I didn't know the name of the chords, but I was playing like an expert. See, rhythm in my hands. Had the rhythm.

Now, this Chinese guy, Scolley Tseu, was the leader of the band known as Scolley's Moonlight Six. He said he was looking for a piano player, and he came over. And I says, "Play in an orchestra? I don't think I'm fit for an orchestra." Well, I played, but I played by ear. I wasn't old, you know. I was still in my teens.

He said to me, "Get on the piano. I want to listen to you playing." He gave me one song, and I played it. He says, "You good enough."

"Good enough for what?"

"Tomorrow night."

"Where?"

"Armory Hall."

Oh, I'm in the big time, see.

Oh, the young people came from all the four corners of Oahu. All nationality. All those who dare to go into Armory Hall, and those who wanted to dance. And they have bleachers all around. The Armory Hall is where the State Capitol is now. Was a large Armory Hall, and that was romantic nights and times. Like the song, "Sweetheart of Sigma Chi," that was one of the songs played over there. So, pleasant memories was connected with that song.

But, you know, I had no idea that playing music for a dance hall is a job, and a job, and a job! So you start at 7:30 at night, and you don't get through till 12:00. No more breaks like we have now, see. Seven-thirty, 8:30, 9:30, 10:30, 11:30. Almost five hours of continuous playing on the piano. My poor fingers! Man, I couldn't feel anything . And yet, I thought I was big-timer sitting on that stage there —half the time I was not even hitting the chords. They yelling out all kinds of songs to me. But I hung on to Scolley and learned more, and more, and more.

You see, the good piano players would take better jobs. From 7:30 to midnight, if somebody else was paying eight, nine dollars, you might as well go and take those other jobs, eh. But with me, three dollars a night, and I'm learning on top of that. My poor fingers used to be so sore. But I played. This was an opening of another world for me. You see how kind my fate was and how the people that I met had a lot to do with my education.

I picked up more music from Scolley's Moonlight Six. And I stayed on with him till I moved away from Kakaako. I later got into another orchestra. Then, I got into entertainment with the Royal Hawaiian Girls' Glee Club. I also got connected with Andy Cummings. All these people have shared in moving me into one line of work or another.

Pretty Soon, Mr. McClellen Was Giving Me Rings

When I was nineteen, I got married to a Portuguese-Scotch boy. He was also a Kakaako boy. His father, Old Man McClellen, came to Hawaii to work on Iolani Palace and was one of the carpenters when they were building it. So, my husband was raised in Kakaako. Then he went to the Mainland, stayed there for awhile.

When he came back, these friends, they wanted Mr. McClellen to have a dance partner, so they call me up.

"Eh, Eleanor, we got a friend. He just came from the Mainland. We want to go Palama Settlement to dance."

I said, "Fine. What is he?"

"Oh, he's half Portagee."

When I hear the word "Portagee," turn me off. I said, "Oh, no."

"But he no look like Portagee. His father is a Scotchman."

So I says, "Well, I'll go out tonight."

So we went. He was a pretty good gentleman and a pretty good dancer. It went on about a year. You know, we go dancing. Pretty soon, Mr. McClellen was giving me rings. See, he's a jeweler. He was just an apprentice, but he was fixing all these things. And he give me ring and he gives me bracelet. What a nice guy. And we became serious.

But, ooh, you have to sneak. You know, I think nearly every household had a daughter or a son that was romancing, who didn't bring their girlfriend or their boyfriend to the house. Everybody was bad. They wasn't good enough for my son, or they wasn't good enough for my daughter. You got to go out and meet him some place. "I meet you at the store." Or "I meet you here." See, this is not good, but this is what went on.

And I was married to him for eighteen years, and then we got separated. But I have three children by him. We're still friends today. One of my happiest life was married to Mr. McClellen. And, later, I married Mr. Heavey. Believe it or not, I've been married to Mr. Heavey almost thirty years. No children by him, though. The children came with Mr. McClellen. And we had a pretty good life.

After I got married to Mr. McClellen, I went to work at Hawaiian Pineapple Company. The wages was sixteen cents an hour. I became forelady around, I think, 1931, 1932. If they like your face, they like your figure, they like the way you pack pineapple, or what, they choose you. But was only seasonal. About two, three, four months the most. Then we got workmen's compensation, which was somewhere around 1938, 1939. When World War II came on, I was on a vacation. Now, when I say "vacation," you can leave, but you don't get any pay. You says, "Well, I'm not coming to work for a whole month." So when you come back, all you do is check in. You're not fired, you're not dismissed. You still got your *bangō,* worker's identification number, and they say you can come in.

December the seventh, 1941 was the blitz. I was supposed to go back to work in December. But when the blitz came on, I said I wasn't going to go back 'cause the gas company was right next to the cannery, and if they blow the whole thing up, you gone. I says, "Who the heck want to go back there and work?" Get blasted to kingdom come. I loafed for awhile. Just feel my ground. Everything was strange. Blackout and all of that came into the picture. Rationing. Go buy your stuff with a ticket.

So I laid low to feel myself, whether we were going to get the hell end of it, or how was it going to turn out.

In about three months, we realized that we were kind of rolling into normal procedures. Then, in about five or six months, they were calling for aviation mechanic students. So I told my husband, "I think this is a better job than going back to Hawaiian Pineapple Company." Hawaiian Pine was still paying only forty-five cents an hour. Just imagine now. Then they were freezing all those who work in different departments. You cannot go anyplace else to work. I says, "To hell with you. I'm going to aviation."

I'm an Aviation Mechanic

They advertise. So, I filled up an application. There was no test, really, for you to fill in. Those days, they needed as much workers as they possibly can get. There was about fifty or sixty of us going to school. You come and learn and get paid seventy-eight cents an hour. So I went down to Dillingham. The school was there. And we learned for about six months or so.

Before, I always feel, "Oh, I'm an aviation mechanic. Chee, that's a big plane. How can I be an aviation mechanic for a big plane?" Ah, but when I started to work, go to school, I learned that for every part of the engine, there's a group of people that takes care of that part. The propeller was one. Your electrical unit, your pumps, each one had their own, see. Then you call yourself aviation mechanic. But if you gave me the whole darn plane, I wouldn't know what to do. I only handle this one section.

When we graduated, ten went over here, ten went over there, ten went all over the place, wherever they put you—Barbers Point, Ford Island, Kaneohe. There were four of us that went to Ford Island—a Korean girl, one Portuguese girl, and two Filipino men. Plus myself made five mechanics.

So, we get there, and people from the whole Mainland, forty-eight states, is over there. So here us bunch of puny island kids, you know, we're not even so intelligent to look at. So, I'm working on my fuel pump, and my other *manong,* or Filipino, friend from Kauai is little further over. My Portuguese friend, she's acting very intelligent, walking all over the place. And I'm looking at all these people from the Mainland. These are all men. Some of them don't even want to talk to us because we're a shade darker. Don't forget they came over here with the same prejudice that they had up there. But we in Hawaii, we've had that before. Nothing new to us. If that was the first time we met them, we would have been very badly hurt. But we've had 'em before, so nothing new to us.

I tell you, the thing that I found interesting when I graduated and went over to Ford Island, was that we were very patriotic. You know, we remembered what the instructor says. "Remember, you are important. The guy that is on the plane is depending upon you to fix this plane on the ground. Once he gets up there, he cannot go out and fix the plane." That kind of teaching. It's true, the pilot cannot come out and fix the plane. It's not like an automobile.

All of us students that graduated, we're conscientious. We worked on our fuel pump, clean it all up, and test it, and so forth. Do everything we learned. Along comes these people from Tennessee, pick up the hammer, *cha-rong! cha-rong! cha-rong!* on this big unit.

I says, "Say, you can't handle that thing like the way you're doing."

"You just mind your own business. I been in this racket for a long time. I know what I'm doing."

So I mind my own business. I keep on a-working. Oh, he's pounding like this. Every time you pound aluminum, you're going to leave a dent, you know. So anyway, the boss catch him. Says, "What are you doing with this unit?"

"What is it to you?"

See, they're real sassy people. We don't talk to bosses like this. We want our job and we want our money. Boss goes back, this guy gets fired. Sent back to his own place.

I worked there almost three years. Those were good years. The beauty about working for the Navy—I don't know if they do it now, but I think they still do—is their system. Outside here, Hawaii had never known of that kind of treatment. Every six months you come up for a rating, and you get a raise, or you don't get a raise. Then if you feel that you are deserving of a raise and your boss didn't give, you can go and find out why. See, this kind of thing, we never had on the outside. We were beginning to learn for the first time that this little rights we're entitled to. You understand? We're suppressed. We kept quiet. No make shame, no make waves.

So, working for the Navy, every six months, you come up for a raise. And who am I to complain when before I was working for sixteen cents an hour? Now here I am working at first for seventy-eight cents. I graduate, I get $1.48. Six months after that, I'm hitting the two dollars bracket. Another six months, I'm up to almost three dollars, see. I never had it so good. This is what happened to the island people. But the Mainland people, who were used to a big money, they were the ones that did a lot of crabbing.

Now, I don't know what happened to the island kids that were working there, whether they had gone back to the islands, or continued in aviation mechanic. For a while, I was going to continue because of Hawaiian Airlines, Aloha Airlines, but I didn't push the thing. I went into recreation field.

I quit before the war ended. It was coming. About that time, the lights were coming on. We didn't have to use too many ration cards for gasoline, and this, and that. All this rationing made a lot of people crooks. They would cheat, black-market, and all that kind of stuff. We had to stand in line for *poi,* we had to stand in line for beer. You can get a case of beer for three dollars, but I'm willing to pay five dollars on the black market.

Then the liquor, we had this Club 99 brand, and all this liquor that Hawaii was putting out. People were buying. So we used to sell it to the servicemen. Fifty dollars for the quart. Was all black market. They dying for drink. All of that went on.

And nearly every night, outside of working daytime on Ford Island, I was connected with the United Service Organizations shows. And the money was good. Some of the shows was right around in Honolulu. Some of them was at the farthest camp. Wherever the men was located, you'd have a two-hour show. I did mostly Hawaiian comic dancing: Hilo Hattie numbers and the "Cock-eye Mayor." Was in great demand, you know. And I think I did pretty good job on that.

During the wartime, there was money galore, but where were you going to spend it? Was rationing. I mean, you couldn't buy anything else, so what you do, you put 'em into bonds. So when I quit Ford Island before the war ended, I lived on my bonds money.

Just Came Out Like Wine

Well, during the time I was living on my bonds money, I was drinking a little bit too much. And I realized it. So my sister and mother said, "Eleanor, why don't you find yourself a job." So I looked in the paper one day and see part-time recreation leader needed. I'm feeling too chic to go in. I says, "Eh, Sis, there's a job over here, part-time recreation. Just the job for you."

She says, "Give yourself a break. Go find out."

So I went in, filled the application, and got an interview along with six or seven people, passed, got the job.

And just around the bend, there was a beer joint. Just around the other bend was another beer joint. Kaneko own one beer joint and Loki owns the other. I work part-time, see. I work from 2:00 p.m. and I'm through at 5:30. If there was a basketball game going on, I'd have one of the teenage leaders take over the game, and I go over to Kaneko's to sit down, have a few. Oh, I think I worked that way for six months.

Well, one day, this kid at Mother Waldron's playground comes over and says, "Miss Eleanor, you know, I like you."

"How come?"

"Oh, when you come over here, we get any kind stuff. You know, you give us the ball. You let us play. And you the best in the whole world."

I looked at him. I'm too shame to go in. Half of the time when I come work, I'm already drinking. I said to myself, "Here is this kid looking at me, and I'm not too sincere about this job. This was just to get away from my drinking that I took the job. Kid telling me how wonderful I am, and I am nothing but a *pilut,* drunkard." Do you know that from that time on, I gradually laid off drink until I quit completely. I came to realize that if I was going to take this kind of job, and this kind of kids was my responsibility, I had to be better than what I was. I wasn't going to continue being a goddarn *pilut.*

So when I left the liquor, my whole being was on my job. This is what I feel the Heavenly Father wanted me to do. So, when I worked, everything within me was all on recreation. All out. I work ten, eleven, twelve o'clock at night, mean nothing.

See, one has to sit down and check oneself. To find out where you going, kid. God who loves you is not going to neglect you. He's going to permit you to see a lot of stuff. Now, you're not stupid. You can evaluate, see. So I've been very thankful with the Heavenly Father, and I've always given the Lord the credit. Because without His power, I'm capable of being very snooty if I want to. When you are humble, you're going to see more for your benefit and for those around you. But when you're high-faluting, you're going to be blind. You see only me, myself, and I. So I've learned quite a lot. And I worked with recreation. So the arts and crafts that I studied, the swimming, the surfing, all of this, all came in use in my recreation years, working with people. Just came out like wine.

Like during the summertime, we had the kids bring all their lunches and place it against the wall, because we'd be out in the yard playing or going on an excursion. When we come back, the kids would come up with their lunch and tell me that somebody took this, somebody took that, or somebody ate the whole thing and left nothing, see. Sometimes kids throw their lunches in the rubbish box. They don't eat it during lunch period or they eat only what they want. So then, I had to tell them the story about my Japanese friend and me.

See, I don't want the kids to go through the same thing as I did. It was so easy to say, "I like a piece of your *ume*." And my friend would say, "I like a piece of your cracker." It would have been so easy, wouldn't it?

I'm always aware of these things that's happening. Like gambling, the same thing. Principal kick 'em out from school 'cause they gamble, and they come into our park to gamble. I tell 'em, "Eh, this is not one casino. You *wen* use that place over there for casino, you come over here for use for one casino. Go take 'em in your front yard and pick up your own money." They "F" me, I "F" them, too. I come from this environment. You know what I mean? This is not going to turn me red. Ain't going to turn me purple. You crazy kid. Hoo, when they hear I come from Kakaako, *pau*. They don't come around and swear at me. I say, "What you think? You think you going turn me red, hah? 'F' you, too. And your mother, on top of that."

But I would like to have been born this age. Not for the drugs. That is for the birds. I feel sorry for those who think that the drug is the only thing that's going to help them work things out. I believe if in case of a problem, you can always talk to someone. I have found this is the best thing at this age here. 'Cause our time, we couldn't talk too much. We couldn't talk to the parents, we couldn't talk to the teachers. And to one another. We always got the wrong dope. Today, you got all your information and facts all in the books.

And the love is growing larger for one another. I believe that it's a Christian love that's coming into being. Once you realize, we can sit down. You look at me as a human being. Not as an old lady. I'm not looking at you as a young kid. I'm looking at you as flesh and blood. Mind, body, and soul. If we do this to one another, we got it licked. Some little thought. Some little warmth. We can do this, 'cause this is our nature. This is God-given nature.

See, you hear the word *'āina*. That word has been the beginning of Hawaii. You understand. I cannot speak of any other place but Hawaiian islands. The eight islands. It is unique because, basically, the spirit, I think, is love of the land—loving one another and everything within it. You cannot love only the river and forget the ocean. You cannot love the ocean and leave the mountain. With all of this, which is most important? What is it? Human being. Everyone regardless of race.

All this time I've been talking to you, you don't hear me talking about myself but the experience I've had, the experience my mother had, the experience my neighbors had from Kakaako. The love for one another, *ka poʻe o ka ʻāina me ka ʻāina*—the people of the land, with the land. Be it in poverty, be it in riches. You love one another because this is where you came from.

That is just a little bit of what I have gone through in life. And as I look back, I say, "Thank you, Heavenly Father. It wasn't so bad."

Usaburo Katamoto
HONOLULU BOAT BUILDER

Courtesy Mark Matsunaga

Born in Nakajima, Japan in 1896, Usaburo Katamoto was the eldest son of Kunigoro Katamoto, a boat builder. In 1910, at age thirteen, Usaburo came alone to Hawaii intending to persuade his immigrant father to return to Japan. Instead, he wrote to his mother, telling her to bring the family to Hawaii. Usaburo became an apprentice at his father's boat shop located at Kakaako and Punchbowl Streets on property leased from Lili'uokalani.

In 1915, the Katamoto family returned to Japan, where Usaburo was married. He came back to Hawaii with his bride in 1920, and opened a shop in Kakaako, building and repairing fishing boats. Because of the high financial risks in boat building, Usaburo left to become a stockbroker. Finding it not to his liking, he returned to boat building in 1924, this time for the Hawaiian Tuna Packers. A 1936 accident left Usaburo with an injured leg, a lifelong disability. He later found work with Inter-Island Steam Navigation Company and the Hawaiian Pineapple Company.

In the wake of the December 7, 1941 attack on Pearl Harbor, Japanese civilians, including priests, schoolteachers, businessmen and community leaders, were arrested, questioned and detained by the FBI (Federal Bureau of Investigation). Among them was Usaburo Katamoto, who was picked up some weeks after the attack. In the 1920s, Usaburo had been vice-president of the Kakaako Japanese Community Association. In addition, Usaburo's brother was a Japanese naval officer and Usaburo frequently entertained his brother's friends when their ships were in port. Usaburo believed that it was due to this "guilt by association" that he was held. Initially taken to the Ala Moana immigration station, Usaburo was later transferred to the Sand Island detention camp. He was one of some 1,500 persons eventually sent to Mainland internment camps from Hawaii. Usaburo was interned in Santa Fe, New Mexico for four years until his release in 1945.

When Usaburo returned, the scarcity of materials, his lack of wholesaler contacts, and decline of the market prevented him from reestablishing his boat business. In 1951, he moved his family to Kahaluu, where he took up farming.

Usaburo Katamoto died in 1980.

At age eighty-two Usaburo was interviewed for the "Remembering Kakaako: 1910–1950" project. Five interview sessions were recorded by Gael Gouveia Mustapha and Mark Matsunaga over a two-month period in 1978. Gael, an ESOHP research coordinator, and Mark, a newspaper reporter and Usaburo's grandson, taped the sessions in a quonset farmhouse at the foot of the Koolau Mountains in Kahaluu. Although Usaburo was very ill at this time, Mark remembered how strong and vital his grandfather had been and recalled how Usaburo, in his seventies, had built a fourteen-foot boat for a friend. Usaburo exhibited a clarity of memory that belied his fragile health. Gael recalls, "He seemed to sense the urgency and importance of recording his role in Hawaii's history."

The narrative which follows chronicles the experiences of this old-time boat builder. The language of the narrative is worth noting. Usaburo, an immigrant, acquired an unusually good command of English which he retained, in large part, throughout his life. Although Usaburo lived another thirty-five years after his release from internment, the narrative and the interviews on which it is based essentially conclude at that point, marking the end of one existence and the beginning of another.

BACK IN MY TIME and my father's time, they had two type of Japanese immigrants. The plantation contract workers stay in certain length of time and go back Japan. Also, immigrants who had contract for so many years for some private concern, like stores, they come, make enough money and go back. That's all one kind. Another kind is you came out here on your own, operating business. That's like my father. He says, "I like to operate boat building." And the United States government allowed that. There was a regulation, so passport was different. First type immigrant's was green; second type was purple. My father was a purple type. And I was called to Hawaii by him, so I get in on the purple passport in 1910.

My father was apprentice to boat builders in Japan, and I was apprentice to him in Hawaii. Usually, apprentice goes in when you just a kid, and sometimes you only carried babies and didn't really learn a trade. But I took apprentice in Honolulu—in my father's shop at the corner of Punchbowl and Kakaako Streets—and didn't have to do any "baby carrying." I did the repairs, building, and collection, too. I was break in real strictly with my old man. And any time, anyplace I look for job, I get the job with top classifications. I was very fortunate in that way. By the time we went back to Japan in 1915, I was a good journeyman.

I stayed in Japan for about five years and came back again to Honolulu in 1920. Only this time, I came back as a married man. But we had no place. Instead of going in a hotel, it's better live in friend's house in Moiliili where they invite us. So we went up there. Stay two, three days. But, see my wife was pregnant, and when she got up from the trip, she laid up. So my friend's mother said, "You better call a doctor for your wife."

I call doctor, he says, "She got the flu. I won't guarantee save your baby. I will try save the mother."

He put her into Kuakini Hospital, quarantine area, so nobody to take care of my wife. Well, I haven't got the money to hire special nurse, so I says, "I'll take care, I'm not working."

My mother's second cousin, Tanaka from Waialua Plantation, was in Kuakini with the flu at the same time. Since the plantation workers were on strike, the husband volunteered to take care of my wife.

I was able to go out into Kakaako and try to collect on the credit extended to Japanese fishermen by my father who built their boats. He had extended about $3,000 to $4,000, but it was a bad time—deflation after the First World War—and no one could pay. I still remember I could only collect thirty dollars out of all of that. It's no use crying. If you can't make it, you can't make it.

So you see, I thought if the man takes care of my wife, I might as well work. I went Honolulu Floating Dry Dock, owned by Inter-Island Steam Navigation Company. The manager was my father's friend. I went up to him and says, "I came back and need a job. I'm broke. My wife in hospital, you know."

He says, "Sure, come out work."

At that time this company did not hire Japanese. The only reason I got the job was because he was my father's friend . The union was Ship-wrights Brotherhood of America. It was a very small union, about fif-teen to twenty men, all originally from European countries—Norway, Denmark and Germany.

There weren't very many men because they mainly took care of repairs. But these men did not grumble about me because they remembered me as a child.

So I start work the next day. I come back to the hospital after work and stay there. A couple of the hospital clerks were my friends from before I left Hawaii. So I have pretty good pulls, you see. They overlook me and don't enforce the regulation, so I could stay there. But they used to joke. They used to tell, "This is not a hotel, you got to get out."

I say, "I get out in time."

That went on for a couple of weeks. My wife was in quarantine for ten days because she got pneumonia following the flu. After that, she was recovering in a regular ward for about eleven days.

And, when she got all right, I figured no stay in Moiliili because I come down to work in Kakaako every morning. No more bus those days. Used to be only streetcar, you remember? I used to take a bike and come down. It's pretty tough. I figured I stay in "Beer House Camp" by the old brewery in Kakaako, I'll rent a house.

The owner of the house made it for two family to live. My wife and I had three rooms—kitchen-dining room, living room and a very small bedroom. At first, we had only kerosene lamp, but later on we had elec-tric light. We had to buy a bed because I did very hard work and couldn't get used to sleeping on the floor. The bed just fit in the bedroom. Toilet was inside the house, because we had sewer system in the area. And we took showers in a semi-public place. We bought all our supplies and groceries from the Fujikawas who had the bathhouse, so we didn't pay anything for the use of their facilities. And the people next door, that was my friends and my father's friends, same time. In fact, we made a boat for them before we left to Japan. They was hard-working fishermen.

At that time, in Kakaako, there were many places, or camps, like ours. On Punchbowl Street there was two blocks like that, too. Each block had about twenty families. And they had one grocery store which would supply the whole area. All kind of different merchants would supply the families. And, everything's on credit those days 'cause that's the only way you can do business. There's no such thing as cash and carry because people, especially Japanese immigrants, didn't have enough cash. And the storekeepers around our area were usually Japanese and some Chinese. You remember, there was quite few Japanese in Kakaako, that is, our area.

But, there were some Hawaiians who used to live nearby, too. Around in front our place there's two house where two families used to live. Below Kawaiahao and around Date camp, just below Queen Street, I can count as far as six families. And between the brewery and Queen Street, there was four or five families. They used to make a living by fishing—*hukilau;* their ground was where Pier 2 is now. Water used to come up to knee-high around then.

But in those days, as far as I remember, very few Portuguese live in our area. 'Cause our area was like a Japanese camp. Most Portuguese lives between South and Ward, more toward Waikiki. They mostly landowners. They bought the land from Hawaiians or somehow got it. As far as I remember, Portuguese usually up Punchbowl, Lusitana area.

But some of them came down to Kakaako 'cause they had draying company, HC&D, Honolulu Construction and Draying Company. Those days, no automobile, no trucks. Whatever they do is a horse and buggy and mules and drays. I remember the company send a ten-, twelve-team mules or donkeys. And Portuguese are smart at handling animal. Yeah, any time we launch a big boat we had those team, and the drivers used to be either Portuguese or big Hawaiians.

So is the lumberyard dealers, eh? Lewers and Cooke, and Allen and Robinson. Those are two big lumber dealers. Their drivers was all Hawaiians or Portuguese. There's no Japanese or Chinese 'cause (laughs) they can't handle animals.

But, they can fish, especially the Japanese. Japanese in Kakaako area were mostly fishermen. The fishermens used to live in Kakaako. Majority. They came from mostly Yamaguchi, Hiroshima prefectures and those days the fishermen fell into different categories.

One type goes after *'ahi.* That's the big tuna. That one class. And there's another class, deep-sea fishing. They fish off the bottom of the ocean. And, there's another type fishermen, aim for *aku* only. These *aku* fishermen that came from Wakayama, a prefecture or *ken* of Japan, was living in town 'cause some of the boat was allowed in Honolulu main harbor—around Piers 15, 16 area. You know, in those days, Aala Market used to be water. And there was some kind of a camp built on the water. Their boat was tied next to the water. I used to go make collection once in a while, so I been quite familiar with them.

I heard during my father's time around ten fishermen get together and scrape up enough cash to buy the boat engine. Because the engine

Usaburo Katamoto and family, c. 1928. *Courtesy Usaburo Katamoto*

cost more than the boat. In some cases they won't be able to put up that much money. The builders, like my father, finance the boat and mortgage it to buy the engine. Then, finish up, let them go out fishing for *aku*. Every week's catch, they divide the money. They take 60 percent for crew and 40 percent for boat owners. That's the way they divide 'em. Crew pays their food expenses during the fishing week. And, both got to look after the boat expenses.

And the cost of the boat, I haven't got any figures to remember that. But you can imagine the cost. During my father time, we used to pay a good man a dollar and a half a day. Not hour, you know. One day. Working nine hours a day. Seven to five. (Laughs) Second-class man is $1.25 a day. That was around 1911–1912, eh. Then, things start pick up and we increase the pay, the good pay to $2.00, $2.25 and $2.50 around 1914–1915, you see.

Sometimes, I remember, we had about eight, nine men. Close to ten. Depends how busy we were. We used to make two, three boat one time, see. But some months is nothing. We just stay on repair yard. And, after that, fuel expenses—bigger the boat, bigger the engine. Cost is coming too much. And, almost doesn't pay. So we try change that to diesel engine. That first diesel, I put 'em in around 1924, I think. By that time, I was operating my own boat shop for two years already.

This was located on Kakaako Street. My father's original shop was next door. When we left to go back to Japan in 1915 we sold it to this man. But when I came back and set up my own shop, he knew he would be out of business, because all the customers would soon be coming to me as they knew my father. So he wanted to sell me his shop, and I bought it. So I owned two boat shops side by side.

In those days, always used to be one, two, three, or four builders. See, one individual can start anyplace. All they do is to get one box for the tools, you know, and they start to build a boat. That's the nice part of it. But, anything more than four builders, not enough job for all. So, one got to give up. They used to come up, goes out of business, come out, goes out, you know. But, at the most, four. Some was by Pier 15 side, but most in Kakaako. You can say three in Kakaako, anyway.

And, the boat builders those days, you can say all Japanese because other nationality can't stand that hard work. And not like youngsters of today who demand so much work, but don't carry on their duties. (Laughs) You know what I mean. These youngsters know what they want. But they don't know what they supposed to do for their rights. Old-timers like me could take it, we worked hard.

If we rush, even big boat, within six months' time we used to finish 'em. It all depends how many men you put on the job. And, of course, the owners want the boat in a hurry. The sooner it kick, sooner it can make money. See, we used to have plenty lumbers then. Not like today, you know. So, we don't have to wait for material to make the boat. But, you might wait for month or five weeks, you see, to get the engine from Mainland. Especially, some of the engine made in the West Coast.

For the fishermen, we build the boat and then we notify after we finish 'em. And they figured we make a boat strong enough. It's very seldom we lost a boat at sea. The government used to send the inspector to check, you know, but they pretty easy on us. They measure, eh? This boat is so-and-so capacity, tonnage, you know, under certain class. And they tell us what to do.

Sampan launching, 1938. *Courtesy Usaburo Katamoto*

So everything was going very smooth, and the inspectors was very easy on us. That way, help the territory's fishing business, too. Brought up too strictly, we won't grow. They very understandable. I think that's the best part of the United States government. If Japan, all government workers go by rules, and you got to follow the rule. But, United States, no. The rules are up to the head inspector and they let us go as far as they can. I think that way you can build up your country faster and more solid. If you only go by regulation you can't do nothing.

Anyway, every time we fix a boat or build one, we make a trial run. Try the engine, power plant, and boat. And we used to take them out Diamond Head, or farther out. A five-, six-hour trial run. We throw out a line and sometimes we catch fish, you know.

Later, when the owners launch their boat, it's customary, they celebrate even they don't have any money. All the friends do it for them anyway, you know. They used bamboo from Manoa valley to put up flags on the new boat for good luck. And, they start make *mochi,* rice cake, eh. They throw that for good luck. Sometimes they put prizes in the cake itself. They get good prizes. Was quite a few celebrations they used to have and usually they put up a tent and throw big party. And, we builders, they throw us in the water. So I couldn't afford to get any good watch. We always get thrown in.

You know, the guys come around and throw me over there in Kewalo Basin. You spend six months and lots of money on the boat, and carry 'em on the carriage to Kewalo. From Kakaako it's quite a ways for us to take the boat on the carriage. We used mules those days. And older days, I remember they had the jackass. They had a dozen jackass on the line, you know. But, still it take too much chances. That one reason why I move the shop from Kakaako Street to Kewalo. When I move to Kewalo, then I build the boat right in front the water. And put boats on the carriage, which is operated by portable radio. Instead of carrying boat long ways, eh, you can put 'em on the carriage, put 'em on the rail and just shoot 'em in the water. Yeah. That's dry dock business. But, we used to call 'em "Kewalo Marine Radio Works."

After doing that for a while, I decide to get out of the boat business. Why? It hard work, you know. You couldn't get skill labor when you need them. And when you take the contract to build a boat, you have to live up to it anyway. So you have to do it mostly yourself. Sometimes, I would work till two, three hours a night. And got to work the following day. Really, it's hard work, and it didn't pay. The Japanese fishermen didn't have too much money. They make a little money, pay living expenses and whatever left over, they invest it in something else. What going to pay for the boat? All that time I got to carry that account. You see? So, it really didn't pay from your business standpoint. And you can't buy no insurance. So all the risk, the builders used to take. That's why it really didn't pay to struggle.

These men ask me, "How much you making?"

I says, "It's hardly any."

So this man says, "You quit the business, and you come downtown work as a stockbroker with me. I think you got more potential there."

Oh, he had big ideas. Of course, he carry through. Chinn Ho—you know, capitalist now—start work in town the same time I start. So we still friend today. Back then, he just finish St. Louis College and came in the office. But I had no school education, or bookkeeping, or accounting, or anything like that. Oh, I fitting as the salesclerk. But, I'm not fit for office work. And in order to sell stocks you got to dress up. You got to do lot of talking, which I don't like, too. You know, sometimes you give them false information—you think it's going to be all right, but it don't have to be that way. Not that I intended. Anyway, I didn't feel that that job suit me. That's why I get out of it. I recall I only did it for about two years.

Then I moved on to the Hawaiian Tuna Packers—dry dock work for them. Build and repair ships, boats. I was pretty good for all kinds of things. Even, I can do part of the machinist work. I didn't suffer any job. And, you see, it was kind of peculiar setup. The Tuna Packers, instead of hiring me by true salary, had to pay me more. In any business connected to a boat I got percentage coming on top of the monthly salary. That was the agreement when I first went in. I took that agreement and it was good, but then late 1930s I got trouble with my leg.

You know Governor [Lawrence M.] Judd? His brother was the doctor the day I got hurt. I was on the smaller boat, and the big tug was tied alongside. And part of the machinery break off, fly up 100 feet and hit me over here on my leg. I could've been killed, you know. Easily. But, lucky just hit and flew out. Then I had to lay up. And they had that big fuss in the company.

The big boss said, "Well, we can't afford to get a sick man on the job. So we going to let him go." The manager couldn't go against the big boss, you know, he had to agree.

So, I left the company. I was out of job for, oh, just a little while—a month or so, I think. Then the Inter-Island, the old floating dry dock, get busy. They ask me to work for them.

I say, "All right. I need the job."

So, I started work for them; I used to work half a day.

They paid me for when I was at work, you know. That was very nice. See, all the foremans and the superintendents, I know them well. And they want to give me a job because they need my service. Well, I gave what I can and when I think I overdo, I rest.

Later, Hawaiian Pineapple Company ask me to refit their tugboat. And, that was the year when war broke out, 1941.

It was Sunday, December 7. Morning time. We were supposed to get first-aid graduation at that Kokusai Theater. The Japanese community—mostly elders—been taking first-aid lesson for about a month, I think. We were just about to graduate so I went to the theater. Then the graduate ceremony don't start because, you know, plenty fires on; they say that enemy plane. We felt that the Japanese attack but we didn't want to say, you know.

Somebody says, "No, that's the U.S. Army taking a target practice." Well, it didn't look like that. It's more real stuff, you know. Then a plane came from Diamond Head side of town and went over the city. It came right over Aala Market which is near the theater. We can see, you know.

Some says, "Eh, that plane don't look like United States' plane 'cause the body is shorter than United States' one. A different shape." We can see that Japanese flag mark on the body. So you know it's got to be real attack.

Then from the police station, lieutenant come over and said to me,

"Eh, you get everybody in the theater. Let nobody go out from there. You stay around here until further notice." So everybody went in the theater, they stuck there and can't go home. Then about, oh, nine o'clock, ten o'clock come, and police honcho say, "You can go now, but we escort you."

Well, anyway, when we get home, just about twelve o'clock. I was having lunch with the family; talking to the kid and my wife about what happened in the theater. Then, here comes a police detective. He said, "Where you were yesterday?"

Well, Saturday night, there was a wedding party in Waikiki. And I was invited. Usually, the party last long time, those days. Twelve, one o'clock. But that night, something was funny, didn't feel good. Among our friends, I say, "Let's go home. I don't feel good."

"Why don't go second party?"

I says, "No, another time. I don't feel good so I'm going home." So we three, four friends left the wedding party together, and I came home about twelve o'clock.

The detective take that down: I was on a party, came home, and sleep early for a change.

You see, Japanese around my age then, always used to have a good time, have a party among themselves—second party, third party until twelve, one o'clock, and dead drunk. You know, those days, there wasn't so many traffic. If we think we had too much, we used to pull up side of the road and take a nap. We kind of sober up a little. Then we come home. We never had any trouble. Anyway, my story true; they didn't bother me for a while after that.

At same time I was working for Honolulu Dry Dock. That's belong to Inter-Island Steam Navigation Company. And, as soon as war broke, martial law start and U.S. Engineers took charge of Honolulu Harbor. I wanted to be absent from work—help the [Japanese] community association. But, I was told, "No, you can't absent from work. We need workers, worse way. You got to work. We need even half an hour work." It's got to be 'cause quite a bit of damage at Pearl Harbor. They send all the small boat to our place. Even a submarine was assigned to our dry dock to be repaired there. And you got to finish 'em right away. They got to put back on duty.

Then the weeks passed and everything was calm down, now. The U.S. Engineers say, "I think we return dry dock to the company and the old union. Finish whatever job you got. Pearl Harbor Navy Yard can take care the rest." So right after the dry dock was returned to the steamship company, pineapple company was getting ready for the next season. The pineapple got to come from Lanai. They don't have tug boat. Inter-Island Steam Navigation Company had the contract to transport pineapple from Lanai to Honolulu. Anyway, we got to come and work again.

And that's when two FBI [Federal Bureau of Investigation] came to the plant and said, "I want you to come with me."

I said, "All right." I was expecting them to call me. I said, "Let me change clothes. I get dirty clothes, dirt, and everything."

He says, "No. You don't have to." After they ask me a few questions. I went FBI office, civilian transportation unit. You know, downtown—Bishop Street above Halekauwila. I went up there.

My wife was there. She told me, "They came and pick me up."

I say, "Oh." I said when they were through with my wife, take her home.

He say to my wife, "You don't have to wait." After my wife went home they start check on me.

They showed me what they holding me for. Had all that papers. And I just glanced at it, you know. My brother was in the Japanese Navy and just pre-war you see, Japanese tanker used to come in quite a bit. Every time they come, why, his friends come and visit us. That's why got to go and entertain them. And they go to parties, you know, and congregate at the Japanese Consul. That sort of records were held by FBI office. They had quite a bit papers typed all out, you know. They say, "We holding you for this." Well, there's nothing we can say about it.

Just about everybody else been getting pulled in, you see, so I wasn't any excited. Was kinda expecting it, you know. As soon as the December 7 attack, that afternoon, they start pulling people in already. From there on, every day, you know, mostly every week, they got so many pulled in. So when they got to me, an FBI says, "Where you been hiding?"

I say, "No, I wasn't hiding. I just been working." I told him I work at the dry dock down there adjoin to immigration station. I says, "My house is up here. Why don't you let me go see my family?"

But he says, "No."

Two, three nights I got to stay in the immigration station. They said they thought they going to release me. I thought so, too, but they didn't. I was sent to Sand Island across the harbor, then shipped up the Mainland for internment.

We head to Oakland where the quarantine island is, Angel Island. We was there one week, ten days. I remember it was pretty cold in the morning, you know. Cooler than here now. They had this steam going on in the room. But, they treat us very nice there, too. Our spokesman was a Southern California University graduate, a man from Hilo. His classmate was in charge in that camp, so there everything went very smooth. They feed us good. They dress us very nicely. I think about ten days we stayed there. But they don't tell us where we go.

They ship us up to Sacramento, through Nevada, past Nevada, and we reach Fort Sam Houston, Texas. We stayed there about two weeks, ten days. Then they send us to army prisoner camp. Cold, you know. I can't recall that place now. But it's in southern part of Texas, near New Mexico anyway. We stayed there about two weeks and then moved to Santa Fe, New Mexico.

The camps had army barracks and as soon as we reached new camp, they organize some kind of a system, you know. They divide us into so many barracks. I think it was fifty in a barrack or something like that. They let us elect barrack captain. And they have a meeting every day, because nothing else to do.

You just try to keep yourself occupied. From a very hard wood we used to make penholder and all kinds of things. We had good homemade tools, you know. They don't allow you so many tools so we take a broken knife, broken steel, and we just spend our time to sharpen it and make it cuttable. You be surprised how they can make, you know. It's everyday work.

Yeah, it occupied your minds. Later, I guess Red Cross donate things like baseball and golf outfit, you know. We used to do that quite a bit. And, like music amusement and that Japanese chess. Pretty smart guys was in there, too, you see. And, we keep ourselves busy if we are willing to. There's enough to do, to learn. 'Cause the only duty we have is to keep within the camp clean. That's our regulation, connected to our daily living. We got to do the cooking and laundry within the camp. We get volunteer from among the members.

Outside of camp, they want so much men to work—volunteer, and pay us ten cents an hour. Usually quite a bit of guys wants to go out the fence. Double-wire fence, you know, and guard here and there. You know, you feel more free if you get out of the fence.

And in camp, even though so many men behind the fence, not many major trouble, you know. Some of the kitchen guys steal rice from the cooking pot, make moonshine, and have a good time. (Laughs) But, besides that, it's nothing.

The only time we had trouble was with the roughneck gang from Tule Lake. Mostly they was niseis came back from Japan, eh. They were for Japan and they didn't want to take any orders from officials. So they were sent up to Santa Fe and were kept in a different compound. We had a little trouble there. Some guys, the officials send somewhere else. But they came back in later days. And they realize that they don't get anywhere. Especially as the war ended and the U.S. defeated Japan.

Yeah, when the war is ended, then—I don't know why they did it—but the U.S. government ship us by train to Seattle. New Mexico to Seattle, so, I guess they treat for us to see the United States. Yeah, we seen the South, East Coast, Detroit, Pittsburgh, all those places, up till Seattle. When we got to Seattle, they assign us to Old Sailors' Union's Home, and we used to eat every meal at the immigration station. There's no big kitchen in the sailors' union, I guess. So they provide bus, you know, and take us to the station three times a day. And, same as usual, you know. We was sightseeing Seattle town.

We did that until we came home on small troop ship. Now, that was a tough trip, from north to Hawaii, eh? It was November and there was rough seas so everybody get seasick. But I was all right 'cause I never know anything like seasick before.

When I get home, it was good to see the family. Few of my friends and my kids and wife was waiting at the pier. We shake hand and it was good. But was just—nothing special. We expected all those things.

The only thing I felt was that we lost a good three years. In fact, three years and ten months. Almost four years, eh? When I come back I see all my friends made big money and sitting pretty. During the wartime, they all was willing to work, you know. They made easy money and sure made good fortune. But, I was out for that time.

Let's see, I got back in November. Then, I was thinking going back to my own boat building business again, but the materials was limited and the wholesalers don't supply new openers like me. They got to supply their own old customers. So I says, "I no sense open." My boat building days were over.

You know, before the war, I was intend to go back Japan. See, my first son was there already. But after the war, the idea going back Japan is out already. From then, I decided what I got to do is to make my own living house here. So I bought a house in Kaimuki. Then after all the kids finish university I bought a place over here in Kahaluu. By then, grandchildren started come out. And I think it's a good place to bring up kids. No cars and clean air. So, we start living in Kahaluu until this day.

III
On the Plantation

Lucy and Seraphine "Slim" Robello

FAMILY, CAMP AND UNION

ESOHP

Lucy Vincente Robello was born in Waialua in 1905 and lived there all her life. Her paternal and maternal grandparents had emigrated from San Miguel, Portugal, with their children Antone Vincente and Mary Texeira Correa, who eventually became Lucy's parents.

Her childhood in the Portuguese camp of Waialua Sugar Company revolved around family, neighbors and the church. At home Lucy learned to bake bread, make sausages, raise animals and vegetables, iron clothes and contribute to other family tasks. The strictness and warmth of a traditional plantation home are evident in her recollections.

Life was simple, yet difficult. People in the community relied on each other in birth, in death, and in life in between. Lucy recalls accompanying her grandmother, a midwife, on trips to deliver babies, and remembers the sadness in a deceased person's home as friends and relatives gathered for the all-night vigil.

There were simple pleasures—eating wild tomatoes her father brought home from work in the fields, a Sunday walk that ended with *manju*, or bean-jam buns, and a shared bottle of soda. She felt that people were happiest when enjoying the good company of relatives and friends.

Lucy completed the eighth grade at Waialua Elementary School. In 1926, at the age of twenty, she married Seraphine "Slim" Robello. She raised their three children and supported Slim's involvement with the ILWU (International Longshoremen's and Warehousemen's Union), although she herself was never active. Lucy died in 1980.

Seraphine "Slim" Robello also was born in Waialua, in 1905. His father immigrated to Hawaii from San Miguel, Portugal with his parents. His mother also came from Portugal, via Boston.

At age twelve Slim started plantation field work during the summers. By age sixteen he began full-time work at Waialua Sugar Company and retired forty-seven years later in 1969. Slim started work stringing electric lines to workers' homes in the camps and running them "open" inside the house for ten cents an hour, ten hours a day. Four years later he was making $2.50 a day, while field workers were still earning a dollar a day.

Slim was an early and active supporter of the ILWU in Waialua. He was elected to leadership posts, took part in negotiations, headed strike committees, and helped to keep the workers united. He was offered supervisory positions a number of times but chose instead to remain a union member.

Slim credits the union for improving the quality of life, especially for bringing a measure of dignity to workers' relations with their supervisors. Yet he was never afraid to criticize union policies when he felt they were wrong. When interviewed in 1976, Slim expressed the hope that the sugar industry would survive in Waialua, for the sake of the younger workers, but was realistic about the sugar industry's declining future.

Lucy and Slim's interviews were part of the "Waialua and Haleiwa: The People Tell Their Story" project conducted in 1976. As the Ethnic Studies Oral History Project's first research project, it concentrated on the lives of people in a plantation community.

The interviews were conducted by Chad Taniguchi, a friend and next-door neighbor of the Robellos' son, Herbert. Chad says, "For this reason, I was welcome in their home and they spoke honestly, candidly, trying to be of help. Mrs. Robello considered her recollections to be nothing special but was glad to share them. I felt her descriptions of the warmth and simplicity of plantation camp life were excellent."

The Robellos lived in a well-kept house with a functional yard and garden. The home was bought from the plantation for $7,000 in the early 1950s. It is cool and clean inside with old furniture, Catholic artifacts (some originally brought from Portugal), and gifts from relatives and friends. Characteristic of the Robellos' home is a bamboo stool bought from Tanabe Store fifty years earlier. The Robellos value their material possessions as reminders of people who have been a part of their lives.

LUCY

Even though we worked harder and all, I think we were much happier before. When we were children we had no problems. Our parents had the problems for us. Everybody would share the good and the bad of the next person. If they were grieving, we would feel sorry for them. We would help them out, and they would do likewise to us. There was a lot of spirit in it, you know.

We had so little then that we looked forward to whatever we had. Now, you have too much so that you overlook even the goods that you should be thankful for. That's the way I feel. The fun is not there. The spirit is not there. It's not like before.

And, that wasn't too long ago. I'm seventy now, but I remember things from when I was about five and six years old.

My grandparents told me they were doing very poorly in San Miguel, Portugal. They heard of the Sandwich Islands—the new country, Hawaii—and they wanted to better themselves. My mother was about eight, and my father was about ten. They came as immigrants on the same ship with their parents.

The sugar plantations here paid for them to come over. I think their work contract ran for three years. Some went back home after three years. But my mother's parents, and plenty of others, didn't go back. They liked Hawaii better and gave up the old country.

They worked hard and helped put this Hawaiian islands into what they are today.

When they arrived in the islands, my father went to Kohala, Hawaii, with his father who became a janitor to the plantation manager. My father had no mother, but he lived with his brother-in-law, sister, and father. And he never used to go to school. The manager's wife asked my grandfather why the little boy didn't go to school. He said, well, he needed the boy home with him. Then she said, "Hereafter, he comes here with you. While you work in the yard the little boy will have lessons." In other words, she tutored him. He learned very well. That's all the schooling he got. He didn't go to public school at all.

My mother went to Waialua with her family. Right off she went to work in the fields. She did it until she was about eighteen years old to help her parents, because the family was big and the wages, small. She used to get, I think, twenty-five cents a day. She didn't go to school either, but here in Waialua there was a Portuguese man that had schooling, and he opened a little night school for Portuguese. My mother only went for three weeks because her parents didn't believe in little girls being out at that late hours. But when she married my father, he tutored her. She learned how to read; but writing, she never did very well. She just could write her name and things that was needed. But she read both Portuguese and English very well. And my father was the one that taught her.

They got married here in Waialua after my father moved from Kohala. My father got a job driving the stagecoach from Pearl City to Kahuku, delivering mail and carrying passengers. You know, he would sleep at Kahuku, and then sleep the next night in Pearl City. He would change horses on his way.

He used to tell us that he liked that job. He brought the more high-class women in the stagecoach and dropped them off at Haleiwa Hotel. I remember seeing the hotel. Was something really nice to see. That's where the royal people and richer *haoles* used to spend their time. They would have some great dances and things over there. That was for the higher-class people. Not like us. We only saw it from the outside. (Laughs)

My father worked the stagecoach up till 1902. From then on, I think, he came to work at the plantation—in the field. Then afterwards, they gave him a *luna,* or foreman, job in charge of a bunch of boys. The boys were tough and had to be manhandled. My father was strong. He could take care of those boys and see that they get to work. You didn't get paid for nothing; you had to work those days. Once, a big rock one of the boys threw hit him. He grabbed hold of that boy, pushed him against the cane car and says, "George, which is better? To be good or to be bad?"

The boy says, "To be bad!"

My father gave 'em another twist by the jaw. He did that about three or four times until the boy yell, "To be good!"

Then he let go the boy. That was one manhandle that I remember he always used to talk about.

It was hard work in the cane fields. When I was a little girl, I remember watching the workers build a cane fire in the night. Then next day the workers would come out, pick up the cane, and carry it to the cane cars. Was mostly Japanese men with their wives. Then my father followed with that bunch of boys to clean up the remaining canes. That was to see that the field was really left clean. With not one waste of cane left.

These Japanese would take the little babies with them out to the fields. They would build little huts out of cane stalks, and the children were sheltered there. While working, they were keeping an eye on the children. Then they would have a hurried lunch and feed their babies. And back to work again.

Poor things. That was dangerous for the poor babies. All day long in the hot fields with flies on top of them, insects and all. And those babies cried a lot, I'm telling you. But the work came first. The parents were getting paid to work. But the poor babies paid for it.

My grandmother was the midwife for this vicinity. She had papers from Portugal and all. I remember going with my grandma on the horse and wagon to different houses while a lady was in labor. And when we'd reach a family home, they'd put me in one back room with their own kids while she took care of that other problem.

The first thing she would do was see the woman. At the same time, the husband would have a chicken all cleaned and prepared so my grandma would have a big pot of chicken soup cooking. And always, in the Portuguese style, there was a gallon of good wine. Soon as the baby was born, that mother would have a nice soup and little wine to drink. No cold things. Whereas now days, give you everything ice cold and fresh. No, it had to be all warm water, warm tea, like that, to drink.

My grandmother didn't get salary for that. The family would pay according to what they had. They paid her with chicken or a gallon of wine; or whatever they have of their own surplus. Eggs and things like that. Sometimes they would even give her enough material to make a dress. They had hardly no money to give, you know.

That chicken soup taste better when it was for a mother with a new baby, you know. I remember my father would take my mother's little bowl with that pieces of chicken and we'd all hang around the bed.

And my father tell my mother, "They have plenty in the kitchen to eat! That is for you!"

And she would say, "These are my children, too. They have to have little bit of this."

And tasted better than the one we had in the kitchen. Was really happy, because there had come one more to the family to feed. You can imagine, the little wages and working so hard. But we didn't think like that. The more children, the more prosperous you was. The bigger the family, the more happier. And that was in all races. The Chinese had plenty, the Japanese had plenty, the Portuguese had plenty.

Had three girls in the family, including me, and had five boys. We didn't have too much blankets, because about two or three brothers and sisters would sleep together. And we had to shut the windows and doors early because we had so much mosquitoes, so that made the house nice and snug.

Our house had a kitchen, and a little pantry to keep the foodstuff. That's all we got. The plantation would give us housing and that was up to us to manage and make it big enough.

We didn't have bureaus or chest of drawers, but each of us had his own box under the bed. We would keep our clothes there. And once a week, my mother would inspect those boxes. We had to have that clothes nicely folded. If it was any old way, we'd get it.

A lot of our clothing came from bags. Rice, sugar, and flour all came in white bags. We would save that for underwear. Our slips and everything was from that. I remember my mother sewing my father's T-shirts. Besides then we would use it for towels. And I remember the 100-pound bags—we'd take at least a good four bags, patch them up, then sew the hem around to make bedsheets. Every bit was saved.

We did our laundry and took our baths in a wash house, which was separate from our house. There was no showers, no anything like that. If you wanted hot water, we used to boil the water outside in kerosene oil cans and carry that to the little wash house. So you couldn't take one nice bathtub wash like now. Hard. Was cold, the water.

We had the big, long table for our family to eat on. My father and mother were at the head of the table. We said grace and we'd put our noses down to the food; no talking. Only my father and mother would talk at the table. If we needed anything, we'd ask permission and we could have second helpings and all, but there was no like you see now, people talking and make such big noise at the table. We ate quiet. My father and mother saw to it that we bring no gossip to the table. That was something quiet and sacred while we were eating, you know. I guess it was like respect or something. Or maybe our parents were so tired by the end of the day that they didn't want too much noise.

My mother did the cooking. She used to make nice meals out of our own chickens, ducks and rabbits. My father saw to it that we had plentiful all the time in the backyard. We were kept busy, because that gave lot of backyard work, you know. All the kids would work taking out the feathers, helping my mother cut the chickens, and all that. She would prepare it. And once it was cooked, it would last long time for us to eat.

My mother never ate rabbit, but she would prepare it very nicely. The day we'd have rabbit, she'd eat something else. My father did the cleaning, but he put me into the job. I used to hate to clean rabbits, but I got to the point that in five minutes, I skin one.

And anytime the fish peddlers—mostly Japanese women—would come, we had fish, because Portuguese like fish. The peddlers had the fish box in the back with chunks of ice. They would put 'em in a scale and you would buy what you want. Mostly was *akule, 'ōpelu,* little fishes like that. If it was a reasonable buy, my mother bought plenty and we'd have fresh fish that day. We had no refrigeration, so the rest was salted. When the Japanese peddlers didn't have fish, they'd come with head cabbages and sweet potatoes, and we'd buy. But everybody had a little home garden for Chinese cabbage and lettuce and things like that. Swiss chard, beets and carrots. My father was great for that. We had that all in the backyard. And we had rows of bananas planted. Papayas and our own oranges.

Then, twice a week, my mother would buy fresh meat. The peddler from Achiu Store used to come on little horse and wagon and deliver meat already cut. When he get to your door, you take the piece you like. At another store that was more modernized, we would go there and buy what we want. He would bring out that big piece of meat, put 'em on the chopping board, and cut whatever slice you want. My mother would prepare it whichever way. Sometimes would be roast, sometimes would be steaks or stew. But the rest of the meat was packed with Hawaiian salt and put away in big crocks.

Pork was the same way. We never did raise a pig, but lot of families would. When they kill the pig, they'd keep half for themselves, and the other half, they would sell to the neighbor or whoever would want.

We'd make sausages out of the pork, like blood sausage. I don't like that. Ooh! (Laughs) Then, we had the pork sausage. My mother, when she pickled the pork for sausage, would cut it in about one-inch cubes. And get enough fat and enough meat; about half and half. You put a little garlic and a good dash of vinegar. If you prefer your sausages real hot, you put plenty hot pepper in it. And you marinate that for a whole night or whole day. Then you stuff your sausages in guts and smoke that in the smokehouse for a good two or three days—slow fire with smoke. We used to preserve it that way, because we didn't have iceboxes. When the smoking was finished, my mother would pack it up in crocks and cover it with lard. Then she'd get a clean hook to take out whenever she needed, take off all that excess fat, cook the sausage, and we eat 'em.

We had our own oven to cook our bread. But, when my mother was a girl they had a great big brick oven that four families could cook at one time. Everybody would be there at the same time, and they would knead the bread and make the dough to make use of the whole oven. For the breads not to mix up, you had a mark on yours. Afterwards, in my time, everybody made their own little oven in the backyard. You

Baking bread in stone oven. *Courtesy John E. Bowen*

could cook when you felt like it; you didn't have to wait until you were
short of bread. The plantation delivered firewood for an oven on horse-
drawn wagons.

As a little girl, I remember helping my mother with the bread. The
night before, we'd make the yeast, which was already a piece of dough
from the last time you cook bread. We take that piece of dough and add
a handful of flour, some sugar, a pinch of salt, and a grated potato. Put
'em inside a jar and mix it all up and cover it. That would ferment during the night. The next morning, early, you'd put your flour, that
whole jar of yeast, and a little handful of pork lard in your pan and
knead your bread. If you had surplus of milk, you'd use milk. If not,
you use water. And not too much sugar, not too much salt. We used to
help her make the little loaves. And then, you'd let the dough rise up.

When the oven was hot, Mother would throw a handful of flour in there. If it would burn, well, was too hot. Had to be just slightly hot so the flour would only brown. Then, the oven was ready for the bread. After forty-five minutes to one hour, the bread would be done. Used to look so nice and brown, the bread.

Twice a week, she used to cook about seven to eight bread. In those days yet, we never used to eat rice. But afterwards, we adopted the rice which we liked more than the bread. And so didn't have to make as much. Maybe about five loaves only. But we were always ready to eat bread. We never gave it a chance to get old.

Besides helping with the bread, we had to see that the dishes was all washed and put away, ready for the next meal. We divided the chores amongst us kids, and as we grew older, Mama trained us. We could do our own laundry—the girls especially. And then we had to take care of the ironing. I remember the charcoal iron. Had a handle and you lift it up, fill 'em up with charcoal, light it up, and when those coals would burn, it would naturally heat up. You'd have to keep on blowing that coals to keep it burning. When you had it hot, you take a piece of wax or candle and wax the whole iron so that it wouldn't stick on the clothes. And you would have to have it at the right temperature, other-wise you scorch whatever you will be ironing. My older sister and myself did a lot of ironing after school for the plantation supervisors. Mostly Scotch people. They had their khaki trousers, all starched.

Once the chores was over, and if we had our homework done, we were ready to go to bed because nothing else to do. My father and mother got up early. He'd go to work. She prepared breakfast for us children, and we'd get up and eat and do little things that we had to do before going to school. That was real early, because school used to start about 7:30. I remember certain times of the year when it was really dark and we were walking to school.

Those days, school was very different. Everything was very, very strict. If I'd say a bad word and you go and report, then I had it, you know. That's the way it was. We had to know how to respect ourselves in school.

And every day, as we entered the classroom, the teacher would look at our fingernails and hands. If you were dirty, you'd get it with the ruler, and be told, "Get out and wash your hands before you come inside the classroom."

It was very common in those days for us to have lice. The girls had long hair, and we didn't have nice bathrooms to take a bath. We'd play rough and tumble, and one lice would get into another guy's head.

That's why my father kept his boys with bald head all the time. And us girls, every day my mother would inspect our head to see if had lice. Take 'em out if we would have. I guess the other parents were doing the same. And once a week, the teachers would inspect us, too.

All us kids took our own lunches. The Japanese used to take their little rice balls with an *ume* inside and some turnips, a little piece of meat, or something. And us Portuguese used to take bread with cheese inside or with butter and jelly. Sometimes we used to change with the Japanese boys. We like the rice and *ume,* which we didn't have. And the Japanese didn't have bread and jelly, so we used to change with them.

When we went to school, we made friends with other races. But once we would come home, we spoke our own language, and the others did the same. The Portuguese all spoke Portuguese. The Japanese with their little Japanese language. And so was the Chinese and others.

We played in our own little villages, or camps, where we were brought up. And the Japanese stayed to themselves. The Japanese was different. Right away, they started making Japanese-language school for their kids. The Japanese kids would come out of our public school and go to Japanese school. They had it right at the church there. The Portuguese never started something like that.

And the *haoles*, they was always by themselves. They always had the best. We wouldn't go over to their place and play. We weren't allowed. I don't know. We weren't comfortable. They didn't like us. They didn't want us there. That's the way I felt. They kept to themself and had parties and things like that, but didn't invite the lower-class people. The ladies played bridge and things like that. We never saw that in our race, you know. We never had that. But now days, some Portuguese people and Japanese play bridge and all that together. Because they have that education—the schoolteachers and nurses and things like that. But not before.

But my father had his Japanese friends, like Tanabe and Nagata. He was very friendly with the men in three Japanese families. And the *manju* man, too, which I forgot his name. My father was a great one for take us children out for walks, give my mother a rest on Sundays. We'd always end up in the *manju* store. For twenty-five cents, was one big bag of *manju*s, buns filled with sweet bean paste. He'd buy that and a bottle of soda, and we'd all share that big bottle while we were going for the walk. And he'd bring my mother her share of *manju* to eat at home. We liked that. Was good. Now you don't see those *manju*s. Even buy them in the store, they hard and not like the ones we used to get.

We used to look forward to my father coming home from work

because he always brought us some little goodie in his *kaukau* can. He would peel a piece of cane and chop it in little pieces for us to chew at home. Other kids used to run across the tracks and cut their own. That was against the plantation rules, but most parents didn't mind that. But we were not allowed to leave the yard. Once we'd come back from school, we were in a fenced yard. We wouldn't go to the tracks and get it. So my father would bring the cane for us. And if my father would happen to hit the field that had those wild little strawberry tomatoes, he would fill up his can with tomatoes. And we'd love that. That was just like little fruits to us.

Every yard was fenced, so we didn't go from one yard running around here and there. We played in our own yard with our sisters and brothers. The girls had doll houses. We'd always be mamas. As we grew older, we had to learn how to sew and stitch, cook, and all that. The boys played trains. Whoo, whoo! By the evening, they were a mess of dirt. Some of them even would be priests. They would be altar boys, like that. Or cowboys. The boys did all men things.

They would do other bigger things. My brothers would go and work for somebody else, cleaning yard. If they got a little ten cents or so, they would be too glad to go and clean that yard.

And, they bring home the ten cents because the owner that gave the ten cents would tell my parents how much he gave. My father never kept it for himself. He would put it in our name in the bank.

The holidays were always happy for us, because we all got together and there was so much good food to eat. It meant a lot to us. The kids playing together and the old-timers having a good time talking about the old country back home. And there was always some guy who always kept happy with the ukulele playing. Or even the harmonica. Now, people goes to beaches and things like that. In those days, no. We were too glad to be at home and on friendly terms.

On Christmas time, the grocery man would have, for each customer, a nice big bag with one apple, one orange, one tangerine. A good amount of walnuts, almonds, and nice little bag of candy. He'd give us that bag for pay back for the whole year we bought things over there.

My mother baked her batch of sweet bread. Now you eat sweet bread every day, because the bakeries make and all. But in those days, would only be the special days.

Christmas was good fun. We all waited the whole year round for goodies. Portuguese always had chestnuts that you have to boil or roast. And then, in the afternoons, was some kind of entertainment. There were good string entertainment. And the old-fashion accordion. The men and women would get together and sing songs. Some went as far as making masquerades and lot of noise and all. Was nice clean fun. No bad things, you know.

Once a year in December, we used to have a feast day, the Immaculate Conception, at our church. For a whole week's preparation, the men would put up booths. The plantation managers would furnish lumber and even supply carpenters. The feast day used to start on Saturday, after work. The men would help with cutting meat and everything. The ladies would prepare and sell food, including lots of bread and sweet bread. We prepared for this event all year long. We crocheted things, did our silk work and all that. We'd give all that to the church, and they would auction that. If they still had things left over that hadn't been sold, they would auction them, too. Rabbits, chickens, pigeons, leftover sweet breads or Portuguese bread. All the little goodies. The money would help the church.

Saturday night, we start having fun. Our fathers and mothers were too busy doing that preparation, so they weren't watching what the girls and boys was doing. We were supposed to be helping, too. But, we found time to have little good time with our boyfriends and girlfriends. We always saw to it we would have a new dress, new ribbon for the hair, new shoes. Was lots of fun. They had the band to play for entertainment. No radio those days.

Then early Sunday morning, we would go to Mass. They would have a procession. Four able-bodied boys or men would carry the saints' statues on their backs. A Portuguese marching band would lead the procession around the block, come back, then put the statues back into place in the church.

Even funerals, those days, was different from today. We didn't have mortuaries and things like that. The family would keep that body home the whole night. They would give the body a good washing, Put the clothes on, and fix them up. Certain neighbors or friends would come and stay with the body until the next day.

They had little coffee and sweet bread to keep the people awake. A leader would say little prayers now and then, and you would follow. Then somebody else would take their turn. There would be peace and quiet after that, because they couldn't be praying all the time. It was just like keeping your company with the family that had lost a loved one.

In my days, people were so poor. They used very cheap candles, like paraffin, three on each side of the body. And us kids, we would be watching around. Those candle drippings would fall on the side. We'd clean up those drippings and put it in our mouths and chew it like gum. And nobody thought anything about it.

And the coffin, nobody would get one from town. The plantation would make one for free. The relatives would all cover the box with a piece of sheet or something. For adult, would be black sheet; for a younger person, would be white. They would carry that coffin on their backs. Was quite a distance from the home to the cemetery.

I think the Japanese have a custom. The families used to put little dishes of food and something to drink on the grave. That's the same with us. Only we don't put it in the grave. We give it to another human being that will eat. I remember going to the Japanese graves on Sundays on our little walks with my father. If we see some nice fresh *manju* or things like that, my father would say, "Look. You folks feel like having that, you eat it nicely and say a prayer for that person, because that's what it's there for. That's for him to eat. And if we eat it in his name, he will be happy." We did it, but only with my father's permission. We'd pick up an orange. Not apples, because I think Japanese are not for apples. But they always had orange in their graves.

I got married in 1926, when I was twenty. That was old, already. Normally, the boy at most would be about eighteen when he was ready to be married. And girls from fifteen up to sixteen. I remember my oldest sister got married when she wasn't quite seventeen. But I hung on a little longer until I was twenty.

Was funny, you know, those days. You just made up your mind that you weren't going to be left a spinster. That would be a disgrace. People sort of look down upon you. They felt, well, "She's no good," or "Something must be wrong with her. The men don't care for her," and all. Whereas now, we don't think of a thing like that. In fact, sometimes we think you better off if you don't get married. But not in those days. In those days, you had to have a husband.

I knew my husband, Slim, from childhood because we went to school together. Was only three months' courtship. There was no waiting around. If you're going to get married, you're going to get married. And that's it.

Oh, our courtship was very strange, I'm telling you. We weren't allowed to go out anywheres alone. One of my younger brothers had to go with me like a chaperone, you know. (Laughs) We were just like jailbirds. Had moving pictures once a week here in a very tiny picture house down by the mill. And we didn't go all the time. My father allowed us only once a month to go. And when Slim would come to visit, my folks saw that I always had something to do in the kitchen.

And he would sit and talk little while. Even when he came to ask my father permission to marry me, I had nothing to do with it. I sat in the sideline and my father and mother did the talking.

We got married on a Saturday afternoon. There wasn't anything too big. Normally, they have big parties when it was a wedding, like how the Japanese old style was. But not my father. He made it a very quiet and little cheap wedding; just the close family members came. And what he saved on not having a big thing, he gave to us to start out our lives. Which I think was better.

Everybody would go to the church, attend ceremonies there and come back and eat. We didn't have to pay caterers like we do now, you know. It would be done all at home. Of course, the parents would buy all the foods, but neighbors would help with whatever we were going to eat. Everybody would do something, which made it easy. And there was always somebody that played either the guitar in the Portuguese fashion or the old-style accordion. And they would sing, make merry.

And at a good regular hour, the bride and groom would, naturally, go home. We didn't go to our house, because the plantation hadn't finished making the little place that we were going to be. In those days, the Haleiwa Hotel had little cottages. We rented a room over there. When our house was ready, we moved in.

Life went on. I had my children. My husband kept on working for the plantation. Then he got involved with the International Longshoremen's and Warehousemen's Union. I never partook in anything like that. It was more of a man's job, and I'm not a person for getting too much into gatherings and things like that. You have to have a more outspoken person, so I let him do the talking. I let him attend those things. I found enough to keep myself busy or active right at home raising the kids. Or I did other little things I wanted to do.

But I felt the union was important enough. I didn't have no objections about the union.

SLIM

When you're involved in union work, you have to have understandable wife. You get up in the morning, you go out. And sometime you don't come home for lunch. You don't come home for supper. And you come home ten, eleven o'clock at night. By the time you come home, the kids are all asleep. You get up in the morning and you go out again, they still sleeping. You hardly see them. And if a wife doesn't understand, then you can have a lot of trouble, you know. And especially '46, we were green. We didn't know a thing about union. So I worked really hard.

And nobody can tell me if it wasn't for the union here in the plantation we'd be making the same pay, same working conditions, and fringe benefits we are having now. Even supervisors wouldn't be getting what they are getting today. They owe that to the union. Some of them don't realize that. But some do. It would be miserable to be working on the plantation without the union. I'm not afraid to say this. This is just the way I feel.

I worked for the plantation close to fifty years. I started working for Waialua Plantation in 1922, as an electrician. I didn't do any field work or anything like that. Stayed on the electrical department until 1969. On different branches, of course.

We went out and wired all of the plantation homes. Those days, even if you had a manhole, you didn't go and do the inside wiring. Did it all outside. Open wiring. I also climbed poles, strung power lines down to houses, and everything. In 1922, I was making ten cents an hour, ten hours a day. Then we got two Japanese boys and about four Filipinos to come and do the wiring. Of course, I gave them instructions and everything.

So, I was responsible for all the wiring and the men. And I was making ten cents an hour and they were making ten cents an hour. They didn't give no consideration about, "Well, he's running the job and I think he should get more than that."

It stood that way up until 1924. That's when the new manager came in. The first manager was an Englishman. I thought by having a Scotchman it's going to be worse, but it didn't work that way. I got a 100 percent raise from the new manager. Twenty cents an hour. So I thought, gee, that was good. By 1926, when I got married, I was making two dollars and a half a day. Field work was dollar a day. But some of the field work were on incentive rates. The reason they put the field work on incentive rates was if you going to pay workers just straight work, they wouldn't produce like they would on incentive. Incentive rates, the more you put out, the more pay you make. But it really didn't make much difference in pay.

And those days, if you had any grievance, there was no grievance procedures to follow. You had to take it whether you liked it or not. They had some real hard head supervisors here. A lot of them had the habit of not calling you by your name. "Hey! Come here!" But we stopped that. After we got organized, management said, "People, they have names so if you want to have anything to do with the individual, you call 'em by name and tell 'em just what you have to tell 'em.'' That actually happened. We brought that up at the meetings of top level management to make that correction.

But before 1945, you couldn't even say one word about union. In the early 1920s, there was a guy who came around on a bicycle trying to organize. They used to call him IWW—"I Won't Work." [IWW actually stood for International Workers of the World.] He was white. He must have come away from some place, trying to make a fortune for himself. As soon as he came around to talk, if management found out about that, he'd get out of there before he had a chance to say very many words. He couldn't sell us. That guy didn't last long, boy.

When the longshoremen got organized, they were talking about organizing sugar. Well, Jack Hall said, "No, it's impossible." The power that the Big Five had, he said that it was impossible to organize sugar. But finally, they came around when Mike Nagata and some of the other boys said they were going to organize sugar. And there wasn't a thing the companies could do. President Roosevelt made it law that you could get organized. And they couldn't fire you, just trying to get organized. Finally, they start signing up the guys. When [John] Midkiff, the plantation manager, found out about them getting organized, he had no choice. If Waialua would not want to be organized, the longshoremen would boycott Waialua Sugar. Would be worse then. It would come to a point that the plantation would convince people to join the union because I don't see how they could operate when the rest of the sugar industry was unionized and Waialua not. So he had the boys up his place. Had a big beer bust and all that. I didn't go, but he said they could get organized, join the union, but he would want to see Waialua be the last plantation to get in. That's actually what happened.

So, around 1945, the thing start getting real hot. The main thing was to get organized.

One particular guy told me, oh, he don't want to join the union, because the ILWU is trying to break up the sugar industry. So I say, "Okay, that's your feeling now. But whenever there's a cane fire, all of the guys and lot of the union members try to put out that fire. So if we are trying to wreck the sugar plantation, you think we'd try to put out the fire? If that's the attitude that the ILWU had, I would let them burn the whole thing down. But we went out and helped the company put out the fire." And a few other examples I gave.

Finally, he consented to join the union. I guess there was more than one that had that feeling but they didn't come out openly. I didn't have an idea what made them think that way. But there was quite a bit of talk that ILWU was Communist-dominated. I didn't believe that. It was never in my mind that they belong to the Communist Party or they were trying to destroy the sugar industry and stuff like that. When we organized, my feeling was that the ILWU wanted to get better wages, better working conditions, better places to live, and, well, to better the workers' life.

Then 1946, came the first strike. I was picket chairman for our group. Because that was the first strike, we didn't know exactly what the company's position would be or how long it was going to take. So all we did was go out on strike and fight it out. Of course, to make up your pay for that three months takes quite a long while. But if you only going to think in that terms, well, you'd never have improvements.

Well, the guys start kind of getting uneasy and want to go back to work and stuff like that. So we had meetings, try keep 'em together. Explain to them how negotiations was going, ask them to sacrifice.

I know one case, a lady came down to the union hall and she start raising Cain there. The husband had to go to work.

So I said, "Okay, if he has to work. You folks cannot afford it?"

She said, "Yeah."

So I got him a job in the millyard punching clocks. And to keep things quiet down, we gave him all that he earned [instead of deducting a portion for the strike fund which was the established policy].

Then a few weeks later, he came back, he say, "Oh, that job is too tired, because you got to walk around all the time."

I said, "Well, I don't have anything else for you to do. So you either take that or you go back home and take care of yourself."

Things like that. But we always try to pick the guys that were most financially hard up.

I think management was really trying to test the union's strength. Check what kind of a union we had and how we could hold it up. But to tell you the truth, I wouldn't want to see a strike go on for six, seven, eight months and then get the cane all burned and everything. Everybody's going to suffer then. But if you can have a settlement without a strike, that would be wonderful. Because a strike's a hardship, not only for the companies, but for the workers and their wives and kids.

But, I thought it was worthwhile going through that 1946 strike. There was very little respect from management to labor before we got organized. Now, if you treat it right, labor going to put out what they supposed to put out. And, I give management just as much credit as I give the labor. Because they're the ones that going to lose out whether things work out or not. Of course, the laborer would lose their job and stuff like that. But money-wise, management loses, too. So I think management has a lot credit to be given to.

I'd rather see sugar business going here for good in Waialua. Keep on going until. . . . I don't know, they say the end of the world is coming pretty soon, but I don't know. (Laughs)

I think Waialua is in pretty good shape, the sugar. I think if Castle and Cooke decides to discontinue sugar business in Waialua, they have to be losing quite a bit of money. I think while they're still making a reasonable amount of money, they're going to continue raising cane. For the amount of money that they are putting in for irrigation pumps and converting from irrigation to drip irrigation, they're here to stay for many, many years. That's my opinion. And improvement of these cane cutters and haulers and new cleaning plants and all that. They wouldn't be throwing millions and millions of dollars if they don't expect to stay for a long time. But conditions might worsen. And nothing is going to stop them from saying, "Well, we're going to go out of sugar business." I wouldn't want to see that happen. I only have a few moons more to go, but I'm thinking about these younger guys.

Back when we got married, we worked hard, money was less. Cost of living was way, way lower than what it is now. Now you have cars. You have a better home. And you have more recreation. All the necessities that you need. And the children are all grown. The best years of my life, I think, was from 1969 up to now. My retired life.

The way I'm living with my family and all, I'm not unhappy. You have your ups and downs, but you got to try to make the best of it. We get along damn good.

Adam Holmberg
A WORKINGMAN'S STORY

When Adam Holmberg was a child, his Portuguese-Swedish father moved the family from place to place. Adam managed to complete the fourth grade of school in Hawaii before leaving with his father, mother, and sixteen brothers and sisters for the Philippines, where his father became a steam plow supervisor. In 1926, after five years in the Philippines, they returned to Hawaii.

At the age of fifteen in 1926, Adam got his first job at Waipahu Plantation as a plowman for seventy-five cents a day. The following year, he moved to Waialua Plantation and worked as a garage man, field worker, camp repairman, and locomotive brakeman.

The numerous job changes reflected Adam's disenchantment with plantation authorities, the difficult working conditions, lack of advancement opportunities, and low wages. These conditions caused many laborers like Adam to seek other work and lifestyles away from the paternalistic and closely-supervised plantations. In 1940, after fourteen turbulent years of open confrontation with plantation management, Adam quit and found a civilian defense job near Honolulu. At the outbreak of World War II on December 7, 1941, he was working at the U.S. Naval Shipyard.

Adam retired in 1972, and today uses his skills as a mechanic, helping at a Haleiwa service station. In 1976, wearing coveralls and sitting in the easy chair of his modest Haleiwa home not far from Waialua Sugar Mill, Adam recalled his "young stinker" days with interviewer-researcher Gael Gouveia Mustapha.

Large and raw-boned with warm eyes and an infectious smile which betrayed his gruff exterior, Adam occasionally slapped his knee during the interview to illustrate a point. His hands bore the markings of a life-long workingman.

Although much of Adam's story is one of bitterness toward his plantation experience, it is also one of a man constantly striving to better himself. While on the plantation, Adam sought jobs requiring more initiative and responsibility. He finally left when his needs could not be fulfilled. Through these efforts, he views his past as one of accomplishment and his story is a positive affirmation of work and working people.

COMPARING LIFE of before and life of today, I would say it's 95 percent better right now. Me and my family struggled in the old days on the plantation. I made $1.37 a day. I go to the store and buy a bag of rice for three dollars, very cheap. But, I had to work three days to buy that bag of rice. You go buy a pair of working shoes for three, four dollars. So it's cheap? So what? That's another four days less of your pay, you know.

Now, I'm retired but just assuming I was still working. On my job, I would be making almost nine dollars an hour. I could buy three pounds of the best steak, have that for supper with my wife, have my car tank filled up with gas, and buy a few more things before I eat up that one day's pay. My pay would be over fifty dollars just for that one day.

That's the very big difference between before and today. A man can go to the store and buy because he don't have to worry: "Oh, shucks, I only got two dollars to spend."

Lot of people tell me that nothing beat the old days. But, anytime anybody mention that, I just tell 'em, "You full of baloney."

You see, my father is half-Portuguese and half-Swede. My grandfather came from Sweden, worked on a Kauai plantation, and got married to a local Portuguese girl. But, from what I gather, he got killed on the line of duty. There was a big cane fire and they got all the workmen to go up and put it out. My grandfather, a sugar boiler in the mill, went out to help, too. And, from what I can gather, he fell in a ditch, with all that smoke and all. He fell backwards and got stuck in that ditch. The water was running over him and he drowned in there. By the time they found him, I think it was three days later. They couldn't find him earlier because he was covered with trash from the cane leaves in the ditch.

And my mother, she came from Portugal with her parents. But, both parents died and she was taken care by somebody else. You see, her real mother died first and then her father got married. Then he died. That left her with the stepmother, who got married again to another man. So my mother had a stepfather and a stepmother. In other words, just like saying two fathers and two mothers.

And, me—I was born in Waipahu but when I was ten, my father took a job as a steam plowman in the Philippines. We stayed there for five years and when we got back in 1926, I went to work, not to school. I went to work for Waipahu Plantation—out in the field, doing man's work and getting boy's pay. Working ten hours a day for seventy-five cents.

Then I came to Waialua Plantation in 1927. My first job was in the garage—taking care supplies, repairing flats, changing tires, and servicing all the plantation trucks with gas and oil. I used to start at eight in the morning, that's when the trucks came in. And, I used to save the afternoons, say, about four until five, only for gassing purpose. You know, the trucks come to the pumps for gas up, check oil, and everything. That was my job.

But I wasn't satisfied with that job. My main thing was to learn some kind of a trade. I tried to get into the floor with the boys to learn mechanic, and talk to the supervisor. But, no dice. The supervisor said, "Yeah, one of these days."

Finally I got so disgusted. I start getting reckless. I say, "Oh, what the heck." So after work, I jump in the truck—didn't have any license, didn't know how to drive—and go bang 'em up. (Laughs) The boss sure didn't have very much use for me.

Then one day, he says, "Oh, we need you out here. So forget what you're doing, come out here, jack up that car, and take off all the tires. Put old tires on because we gonna junk the car. We gonna take 'em down the dump or some place."

Not knowing any better, I went, "Okay." I never work on anything like that before because I was only a supply man. So I grab a hold of four jacks. I jack this wheel up, I jack that wheel up, I had the four jacks up in the air. Really nice job, you know.

All of a sudden, this doggone guy, Portuguese, comes over there, he's gonna get smart, see? He give the car a push. Naturally, standing on jacks, you know what's gonna happen. Bzoop! The car dropped. So, the boss comes over and says, "Dammit, you got your brains in your backside!"

I mean he's insulting me already, you know? I made a mistake, which he should have corrected. Then the other guy had to make it worse by pushing the car off. Well, I got so mad, I told 'em, "Yeah, take a straw and suck 'em up." The boss hated me; from there on he had no use for me. I would never get a job on the floor, because I told him to get a straw, see? I got fired from the garage, and they put me out in the field.

I was making dollar quarter in the garage. In the field, I worked for a dollar a day. At a dollar a day, they called that "day work." But, if you had to go piecework, weeding, they'd pay you by line. One cents, two cents a line. And you have a long line to weed. The supervisors set the price on the line. If it's a good place, with not much grass, maybe you can weed enough lines to make a dollar and a quarter. You might even make 200 lines a day. But, you hit the bad spot, you might make twenty-five cents a day, and they wouldn't give you a penny over that. That's how life was in the plantation.

And, there were the *lunas*, or overseers. The meanest and dirtiest *lunas* you could find were the Portuguese. They were slavedrivers. They wouldn't even steal a nickel from the plantation to give you. If you made thirty lines, they wouldn't pay you for thirty-one or give you a little extra, whatever. No, no. It had to be that way. Everything would be for the plantation. Nothing for the workmen.

I work for Japanese *lunas*. And I consider them 100 times better than Portuguese *lunas*. And the Scotch overseers, above all they were Jesus and God, put altogether in one. That's the reason I'd get fired, I just couldn't take any more.

I was a troublemaker, black sheep of the house. Getting in trouble, being called in the office, and get fired and hired, and all. So finally, the plantation manager called me in and told me, "I really don't know what to do with you. But, I have a plan. You stay away from trouble for six months, do your job without any complaints. Don't do any trouble at night around the camp, and I'll stand on my word. Any job you can handle, ask for it, and it's yours."

Well, that's a good deal. I say, "Okay, I'll try anyway." You know, I didn't know if I could do it because I was a real pest, a termite.

So I worked on picket fences, doing a good job. The day that ended the six months, I went up to the manager and said, "You remember back at a certain date we talked? Today is the day that make six months."

He go look and says, "Yup, that's right. No complaint so far, but anyhow let's call your boss."

So the manager told my boss, "Well, today's the day. Six months. I wanna know his record."

My boss said, "Oh, shucks, he's been good. I never caught him loafing. He worked every day in that six months. And so far, I never heard about him doing any wrong in the camps."

Actually, the guy never know what the heck I was doing. He was never around half of the time, anyhow. (Laughs)

So the manager says, "Okay, what job do you want?"

"Say, I'd like locomotive brakeman."

He says, "Brakeman is yours, but first we have to find out if they need any men."

I say, "Well, from what I understand, they need one brakeman."

"Okay, let me give a call."

So he call up and they say, yeah, they need one more. He send me over to see the locomotive chief. But, he happened to be my neighbor! His kids used to throw rotten mangoes in our yard and hit my sisters. I got into trouble with the kids and finally I had few words with him, you know. I was young and he was an old man. When I hear I had to go work for him, oh my goodness!

The locomotive chief say, "No! You blankety-blank, not with me. I'd rather get fired than give you a job."

I say, "Well, all right. That's all I wanted to know, because I was sent here by the manager to find out if you need a man. He wants me to get into a job, and that's the job I was promised."

"Oh, no! You don't get a job."

I said, "Well, okay, we'll find out." So I went back to the manager. I told him what happened.

He say, "Tomorrow morning, you be down at roll call at five o'clock for get this thing straightened out."

That morning, he got a hold of the old man. "I am the manager. When I says that man's got the job, as long as you have a vacant spot, that man gets the job. Well, think it over now. You either give him a job, or you fired. You take your choice."

Ha, the chief wouldn't want to get fired, with all his years, so he gave me the job. The manager told him, "Both of you don't get along very well. So, if there's any complaint, see me. You don't fire that boy. If there's anything wrong, you talk to me, and I'll talk to him. I don't want you to have anything to do with him as long as he's doing his job."

So I started working in the locomotive department. We used to work ten hours a day, starting at five o'clock in the morning. Our regular job was to take the engine and go around to the camps. Pick up all the labor on what they call a "labor train," and bring 'em down to the mill. Cut-

Plantation locomotive crew. *Left to right:* brakeman Frank Pacheco, brakeman
Joseph Holmberg (Adam Holmberg's brother), fireman John Sergave, c. 1930s.
Courtesy Adam Holmberg

cane men, loaders, and everything else gathers there, and they issue all
the orders for the workmen during that day.

You see, those days the cane was all loaded by hand on railroad cars.
The cars come in, and the workers pick their car. Everybody have their
own car. After the cane is cut, they had women—wives, mostly Japanese
—out in the field piling cane. The men would just grab the piles, run
like heck up a wooden plank to the top of the car and dump 'em in.
You have to hope that you make it to the top before you fall. If you did
fall, that was a pile of cane you lost. Then you start all over again.

The *luna*s wouldn't care too much, if you fell. You see, you were getting paid by piecework—by tonnage. The more cars you load, the more
money you make. So, if you was bit slow on the job, the less you would
make.

They had so much people loading cane that by the time we take a
load down to the mill and take empties back to the field, we would have
another couple of loads waiting for us, and sometime there was no stop-
ping. If there would be a delay—if we had to wait out in the field—we'd
come down to the mill, pick up empty cars and keep working. If we
didn't get the cane out by 4:00 or 4:30, we worked till midnight. Sometimes, we used to work till two in the morning. That's for $1.37 a day.
That's all. Your work from four in the afternoon up till you finish was

free time for the plantation. In other words, you were paying the plantation, not the plantation paying you.

If we had a wreck out in the field—whatever time the wreck would be —we had to work that whole day. Sometimes you work all night. Sometimes for two or three days, you was away from home! I was living right here in the plantation, yet I couldn't come home because there was a job to be done. They wouldn't let me come home and eat. You had to work just like slaves, without even anything to eat or drink.

Finally, a few years after that, we start making a complaint, so they would bring us sandwiches. And, sometimes we would go home, have a rest of two hours and report back to work. Even if you couldn't keep your eyes open—they didn't care whether you were gonna get killed on the job or not. As long as you were there, that's what they were concerned about. I almost lost my job because I refused to work one time, but I had to work whether I wanted to or not.

But, look at it this way—if you work at least twenty-three days a month, you get ten cents a day bonus. If you don't make twenty-three days, you don't get your bonus. And if you don't work twenty-three days for couple of months, you might lose your job.

Worse yet, depression time, when they took our bonus away from us, the plantation was still strict. You had to work, because they needed the men. So if you gonna goof off, they pull you on the carpet. With no bonus, it hurt at that time, but we were better off than some people back in the Mainland. At least we had the plantation to look up to. We couldn't live like royalties, but we still had our food.

If you had a good cook and know how to save, you could make it. My mother was pretty good. Pork was cheapest those days, and she could do a lot with pork. Sometimes, maybe on Sunday, we'd have roast pork, Portuguese style. My mother was Portuguese, so she had the Portuguese way of cooking which my wife still does. And boy, I tell you, that's what we ate and really enjoyed. Then, those days, you had to have a garden. You plant vegetables and all that. That's a big help. But like I said, we used to eat pretty good, especially on Sundays. We wasn't starving.

But it was a hard living. Anyway, I stay on the job, they took care of me, and everything went smooth. Finally, the old man, the locomotive chief, got to like me because I'd go out of my way just to do things, you know, to help him out. But one time I *wen* ask him for a raise. I say, "Eh, Jesus Christ, how come I don't get a raise, or I don't get a promotion?"

So he told me, "I tell you what. I give you my wages, and I'll take your wages, and you take care of my family."

He's not gonna give me a raise, but he's gonna let me take care of his family and give me his wages. That's the Portuguese for you. Typical Portuguese in the plantation.

Our family lived in the Portuguese camp, right by the Catholic church. They had all different camp. You know, they had Filipino, Japanese, Korean, Spanish, and Portuguese camps.

After work, when I was single, we used to go hang around the camp store. That's where all the boys—mostly from Portuguese camp and some mix bunch—gather to see who could tell the biggest lies. Some used to bring their ukulele or whatever and play music. And about nine o'clock everybody split. You go your way, I go mine. To all different branches we go, just like a crossword puzzle. And, the next night, the same thing again.

A few of them used to drink. But was Prohibition at that time, so we drank that *'ōkolehao,* or washtub booze, made from the *tī* plant. People was bootlegging nearby. And even though I never drank the stuff, I used to make home brew. Just for the pleasure of making and bottling it. I was pretty lucky. I never had one bottle explode. The boys would come over and I'd watch 'em drink. Maybe I'd have a shot and that's all. I never was a drinking man. Maybe I drink a couple and then start feeling pretty high.

But, I was smoking. I never did get caught by my parents until finally, just happened that I saw my father coming. I got so excited, I took the cigarette, put out the fire—I thought I did—and I put 'em in my pocket. It burned a hole through, and there was smoke coming. My father say, "You on fire! What happening?" So, he caught me. And he try to get me to stop smoking. But, I already had the habit.

For everybody, that's the only things we had for enjoyment. Unless, we would go movies. But, you see, after making all that money in the plantation, you didn't have very much for movies. (Laughs) At that time, it wasn't cheap. First, was dime, and then when the talkies came out, came up to about two bits.

Yeah, didn't have too much before. But, in those days, the plantation would chip in and they'd make the Fourth of July a big day. In the baseball park, they'd have baseball, basketball, all kinds of sports for the plantation people.

But, usually I worked on that day, because somebody had to go out in the camps and pick people up. Those days, didn't have trucks or buses as transportation. So the locomotives go out, bring the people. We would leave the engines alongside the baseball field and watch the games. When everything was over, we take people back to their camps, put the locomotive back to bed, and that was it.

The only time I used to enjoy holidays was when I was single. Young days, I used to really go and have lot of fun masquerading on New Year's Eve. You put on a mask, a funny kind of suit, make yourself as ugly as you could, and go around from house to house. We used to go all over the different camps. All over Waialua. People would invite you in the house and you have a shot and maybe a fruitcake or something. If you didn't go to somebody's house, then they'd feel hurt, you know. They thought, "How come? This guy don't like me?" Everybody would be expecting you. Not now. You do that now, they shoot you! It's something that's not done any more. Just gradually faded away.

The young kids don't know what we used to do. They don't know what life was. They think life is jump in the car, and get going ninety miles an hour. Maybe go in a bar. You know, that's life now. To kids today, this idea of staying home with the old people is phooey!

So, now, it's all automobiles and motorcycles, and life is moving fast. Those days we never had no such thing. No TVs or anything. So you had to enjoy yourself at home, and try to make it the best you can with the group. But now, the way kids do it, they jump on the car and go.

When I was young, I had an old Model-T car. I was single those days, and the only car you could get cheap was a Model-T. I got a girlfriend in Honolulu, so I start to go to town with my Model-T. Finally, we broke up and I start going with this German-Portuguese girl. After two years and six months, I think, we broke up. Then I start going with her cousin, she was Chinese-German. And, that didn't last too long.

Finally, I made up my mind to get married to a local Waialua girl. At least I know she's there. The girl I married was born and raised in Waialua. I lived less than a thousand feet away from her. I watched her grow up, but those days, I never paid much attention to her because I was always looking for outside girls. Then I started talking to her more, you know. I just got up one day and says, "Well, heck. Might as well." Shucks, before I even knew it, I propose. We got married 1936, in June.

At that time, I didn't have anything, so my father say, "Oh, what the heck, might as well get married and live with us. That way you and your wife can get a start." So that's how we live about two years. We had a big house, so my wife and I lived in one room. But we were all in the family. We eat together and everything.

But three months after I got married, my father died. Then, I had to go under for appendix. And that was money tied up again. No work, no money. After that, we start getting pretty good again. Then I moved from my mother's house to what they call the new Puuiki Camp. By then my mother needed help. So the only way I could help was by taking in one of my brothers. That would be all right. But, then my other brother came, too. He start paying me board, but that wasn't enough. One day, this brother bought a washing machine to help my wife. But, whatever he was paying for the machine was deducted on the food bill. That made it pretty tough because we accumulated a balance in the plantation store. See, you owe your life to the company store.

They told me, "Well, you have a balance here, so now we have to cut your wages down to seventy-five cents a day." Now, that was supposed to feed my two brothers, my wife, my child, and myself.

So, I told my young brother, "You better go home with Mama." I went down and told my mother what had happened. I say, "Sonny have to come back because I cannot keep 'em."

Then I told my other brother, "You better move out and go look for some place else to stay because I cannot keep you." He not giving me enough anyway.

He says, "Okay, then you pay for the washing machine."

I say, "I cannot. I'm in balance already. You take that blooming washer with you. You pay for it. How am I gonna pay for a washer with seventy-five cents a day?"

That's how we lived, for seventy-five cents a day for about a year. That's when my wife and I were having one meal a day. And lucky I had chickens and ducks, and neighbors were giving all the leftovers like vegetables. That's how the ducks was living. Every once in a while, I could squeeze in a bag of middling, you know, something cheap. And the baby, she was one year old, so we had to buy all that cereal and everything else. All that time, we would be living on chickens, ducks, and fish.

So we managed. I kept working as a locomotive brakeman on the plantation. But, in 1940, I left. I got my walking papers.

You know, I had my troubles. Whatever happened in the plantation, when I was young, that's my fault. I admit, I was really a stinker. But, after I settled down, it wasn't my fault any more. It was my fault, plus the other guy's.

See, I left because of a train wreck. I was coming down with a load of cane. This other guy quits work early for the day and stops his train at a dangerous point in front of me. I thought he was going to move, so I slacked the brake. I hit 'em and was a big wreck. Throw all the cars down the gulch.

It wasn't my fault and the thing could have been avoided; it's just that the guy didn't want to move. But, I was always to blame. The new superintendent didn't like me anyway and start blaming me right off the bat.

So I thought, what the heck. Why go cry or try to say it's not my fault and go pleading. The heck, let 'em do what they wanted. I disgusted. I took the blame on that. Then that's when the superintendent got smart with me, and I couldn't take any more. I start cursing him, calling him everything under the sun. I wanted to smash his eyes with his glasses on. So, finally he told me that he didn't want me in the locomotive department any more. They were gonna see if had anything else for me.

This time I was on my own, the nice manager who helped me get the job didn't help me any more. He let the supervisors handle it. In the meantime, I figured I might as well look for something else because I'm not in very good standing in the plantation. So I went to Honolulu and looked for a job. I got one that same day. Then I went back to the plantation just to see what they had lined up for me.

The plantation industrial relations man said, "Yeah, I had a nice job for you. Tractor operator. Makes good money. But, then again, we cannot have employees here on the plantation beating up their superiors. So naturally, we don't have anything for you."

I told 'em, "Well, thank you very much. I just got a job in town that's paying $140 a month, which I never saw in my life for the thirteen years I work in Waialua. So take that wonderful job that you had for me and shove it up your backside. I'll get a board with nails and nail it across your backside. You can have that wonderful job for the rest of your life." And that was it.

So I left the plantation about September, 1940, and went to work as a night watchman at Ford Island. I also took care of the boiler in the morning if the man that's supposed to light it up didn't come. And I stayed on that job for about one year.

Then I left there in the beginning of October. When World War II broke out in 1941, I was working at the U.S. Navy Shipyard.

I remember December 7. Vineyard Street and Davies Lane, that's where I was living. The beauty part of it was that my neighbors was all Japanese and I get along great with them. So does my wife. I had bought from Sears and Roebuck, a band saw and a table saw. So this old Japanese man wanted an ironing board for his old lady. I figure, what the heck, I make her one since I had the tools. So I was working on the board on Saturday. Then Sunday, December 7, I continued.

As I was working, this plane start flying over. All of a sudden, boom! Bombs start exploding. I look up and saw all these planes, you know. I didn't notice that they were Japanese planes. I just says, "Doggone it, even on Sundays, you can't get rest." I mean they maneuvering and bombing the heck, and everybody sleeping.

Then this old Japanese fella came out, look at me, and says, "Eh, Homburoga! Japan come."

I say, "Naw! That's maneuver. American plane. Maneuver today."

"No, no, no. This Japan. See? Japan, America fight."

"What the heck!" I look up again. The Rising Sun! Eh, this is getting bad! So, I told my wife, "*Chee,* something is happening." Something really bad because bombs are exploding right by my house. A guy lost a couple of legs close by where I was living. Bomb exploded, caught 'em, and blew his legs against the mango tree.

All of a sudden, the Navy put in an announcement. "All Navy yard employees, report to the Navy yard, immediately! Do not come by car, but come with the Oahu Railway." They were running a special train because they didn't want too much traffic. So, I put things away, got dressed, and told my wife, "This is it."

When I got down the Navy yard, they were still bombing down there. So, the only thing I could do was show my face. They told me where to go but instead of going there, I went under the lumber pile. I thought I was going to be a lonesome guy, you know, alone. Heck no, I had plenty company! (Laughs) We stayed there until everything quiet down. And then, I went back to my crane.

I wanted to come home to see my family because my children were really small. So when came dark, I walked home because there was no transportation. I walked home with about eight guys. That's the most stupid thing anybody could do because there were guards all over the place. They challenge you and you don't know when you could get shot. And it was blackout. Well, finally, somebody picked us up with a pickup truck with no lights and we got a ride home.

My family were all okay, so I stayed that night. Next morning, I reported to work, and they says, "You supposed to be going home, not coming, to work."

I said, "I went home last night because I had to see my family and nobody told me I had to work overnight."

He says, "You go back home and report this evening." He told me what time to report. So I did.

After that, things went pretty much back to normal. They had the buses running and all that. That's how I went to work because I didn't have a car. But, still you couldn't move around at night because everything was dark. You had to walk around with a flashlight painted blue, and you couldn't see two feet ahead of you with that flashlight. I couldn't do any work. Even if you wanted to work with the crane, you couldn't see what you were doing. Then they get little bit lenient on the lights, and that's when we start producing work.

But, in the beginning, everybody was too scared to move because you never know when you were gonna get shot. Any little noise, and that's it! So what we done mostly was stick around our equipment. When they needed us, they'd call us. We used to even be afraid of leaving the crane to go to the cafeteria. Usually I eat there, but when it was really bad, I took my own lunch. It was really, really rough.

Because I worked at the Navy shipyard at nights, I had nothing to do during the day. So I went to work for Sears Roebuck part-time. Then I left Sears and worked for Irish Cabs as a handyman. Finally, I gave up the part-time work and just stayed with my regular job because I had enough to do at home. My hobby was automotive, you know, mechanic. Then, I made it a business. I had my own repair shop. In my yard, of course, but I had my business license and everything. I used to do my own repairs so that was enough to keep me busy.

After the war, we moved back to Waialua. From the time I left in 1940, I been always wanting to come back, you know, even if I had to commute to work. I used to come up practically every weekend to go fishing and all that. So, I thought, why not live up here? I saw this place in the paper. For sale. So we came up and I took one look at the place, and say, "Oh, oh! This is it. I'm ready to go back to town."

My wife says, "No, our money is running low. We need a place. Let's buy it now."

I say, "Well, I know, but look at the work!" We had plum trees, *kiawe* trees growing in here. Then we had coral heads about three feet high, and about three feet in diameter. You couldn't walk at night through this yard without broking your shins or legs or even your skull. Anyway, she wanted the place, so we bought it. Then we start working on it. While living in town, we'd come up every weekend and haul coral until we were blue in the face. After we got all that done, we rested awhile, then we started with dirt. All that work.

But, it's really worth it. I'm glad we done it at that time, because I was young and strong. If I had to go through all that again, never. Not at my age. Not with my arthritis and everything. I'm on the easy now. Retired. I move when I feel like it and go down to Yama's Haleiwa Garage Service just to keep busy—putt around.

Being retired, I don't make much, but enough to really enjoy. We can still go out and have dinners where we have to spend a little money.

We can afford that. Sure in the old days, you could buy a bag of head cabbage for fifty cents. But who the heck wants to eat cabbage every day? I don't even like it for one day.

Oh yes, it's a beautiful life, now. Really good living. Easy living, you know, you have everything now. No problems.

See, I was planning on having my kids go to college. But my boy wasn't the type for school. The teachers had already told me, "No sense. He's not the type that wanna go to school, so he wouldn't learn. He wouldn't be interested. So let 'em go to work." I didn't expect miracles. And I didn't expect them to be professors, or anything. I expect them to be a workingman like their father, that's about all.

Pedro and Cresencia Ponce
THE STRIKER AND THE HEALER

ESOHP

Pedro arrived on Kauai in 1922, and Cresencia two years later, both young Visayan immigrants from the Philippines. They met during the territory-wide Filipino plantation strike of 1924. Pedro was first assigned to Hanamaulu Plantation, where he did *kālai,* or cutting of sugar cane. Just prior to the strike, he was given the job of irrigation ditchman, supervising nine co-workers near Wailua Falls. In 1924, Pedro decided to join the strike and moved to the Kapaa strike camp located in the Hee Fat building. He solicited food donations from non-strikers and earned needed money planting coconut trees on private land.

At Kealia Plantation, Cresencia worked briefly as a laundress, then as a plantation laborer, stripping and bundling sugar cane leaves. She later joined her sister at the Kapaa strike camp where she became acquainted with Pedro.

Pedro and Cresencia were married at the end of the strike. Refusing to return to the plantation, Pedro opened a barbershop, working for fifty years until his retirement in 1976. During this time, Cresencia became known on Kauai as a *hilot,* or folk doctor. Parents of six, the Ponces made their home in Kapaa. In 1983 Pedro died at the age of eighty-three.

Some 37,000 Filipino immigrants, more than four-fifths of whom were men, were brought to work in Hawaii between 1906 and 1924, about half arriving after 1919. Most were from the Visayan Islands or the Ilocos provinces. As the last immigrant group to work on Hawaii's sugar plantations, Filipinos were paid the lowest wages. In 1924, Pablo Manlapit, a labor organizer and leader among the Visayans, called a strike for higher wages and better working conditions. Pedro remembers hearing Manlapit speak: "His (Manlapit's) talk was that we Filipinos have to pull together, be united, and we can raise our salary." But Cayetano Ligot, an Ilocano labor commissioner from the Philippines, persuaded the Ilocano workers not to strike. Out of thousands of plantation workers on Kauai, only about 600 participated, including women and children.

On September 9, 1924, a violent clash between strikers and police took place in the Hanapepe strike camp about twenty-four miles from Kapaa. Armed police had gone to pick up two Ilocanos at the strike camp, believing them to be prisoners of the strikers. How the battle precipitated by the confrontation actually started is not clear. Outarmed by the police, the strikers fought with cane knives, sticks and a few guns. The toll: sixteen strikers and four policemen killed. The ensuing mass arrest of the Hanapepe strikers left Kapaa as the only strike camp on Kauai. Two days later, the National Guard searched the Hee Fat building for weapons and arrested nine Kapaa strikers after finding two pistols. The remaining strikers were evicted from the Hee Fat building a few days later for nonpayment of rent. Pedro and other strikers collected scrap iron, secondhand lumber and cardboard to build a shantytown on the nearby beach. The strikers' shacks were among the first sights Cresencia remembers in Hawaii. Shortly after arriving, she went to live with the strikers at the camp. On May 16, 1925, seventy-seven male strikers —Pedro among them—were arrested at Kapaa for criminal trespass, ending the strike on Kauai.

In 1978, Pedro and Cresencia were interviewed for the "1924 Filipino Strike on Kauai" project. The interviewers were Gael Gouveia Mustapha, project researcher, and Ed Gerlock, then a Catholic priest who acted as translator. Three interview sessions in the Visayan language were conducted at the Ponces' home, a small, plantation-style house on a Kapaa hilltop. Gael and Ed still recall the hospitality of the Ponces, who were always concerned that their guests not leave hungry or thirsty. Gael describes Pedro as soft-spoken—"a man small in stature but large in heart." She remembers how proud Pedro was of his wife for her healing abilities. Cresencia's belief that her healing power came from God and that it would be wrong to profit from it made a lasting impression on Ed.

Edited from translated interviews, this narrative reflects the thoughts and experiences of the Ponces, sometimes from differing perspectives.

Unlike other narratives in this collection, it focuses on one event occurring within a relatively short period of time, documenting the profound effects of a single historical event on two lives.

PEDRO

"IF I'M STILL ALIVE, I'll be back after three years." That's what I told my mother before I left the Philippines.

She was already quite old, and I was hoping that I could help her live a very peaceful life in a nice house, where she could eat good food. That's really the main reason I came to Hawaii in the first place.

In Cebu, where I was born, I went to English school but only up until third grade. Then I began to help farm the little piece of land my parents had, planting rice and corn and things like that. My parents were very poor so there was nothing that could be done.

Because I wasn't going to school any more and there wasn't that much work at home, I worked for the government, building roads. After that, I didn't have any more work.

In Cebu there was an office at the immigration center that had agents looking for workers to come to plantations here in Hawaii. They were looking for young, unmarried men. If the person was married, that was okay, but, of course, many of them were not married.

I went to the office and presented myself. They examined me physically and found I had no sickness, so they accepted me. This was in 1922, I was 22 years old.

There was a contract that we had to sign. Once you signed it, you had to come here to Hawaii and work for whatever sugar company they assigned you to. If you worked for three years, you could go back to the Philippines. The transportation was free. There were some who fulfilled their contract and went back. Others didn't go back any more, especially those who, like myself, had families.

We who were recruited got on board the *President Lincoln* in Cebu. We were all Visayans. Then, when we stopped in Manila, we picked up some Ilocanos. From Manila, we went to Hong Kong; then we sailed on the same ship for Yokohama. There, we changed to another boat, the *Taiyo Maru,* a Japanese ship. And that's the boat we went on from Yokohama to Honolulu.

On the ship heading for Honolulu, many of my companions got very sick. I think that along the way we must have picked up some kind of sickness. You know, it wasn't a very clean ship and it smelled quite bad. I myself was throwing up. I tell you, the last time I threw up, I vomited blood.

We finally arrived at the immigration station in Honolulu. We were there for one week. The Visayans were not so many because nine had died on the trip. There were only thirty-one left. Some were sent to Maui, or to Hilo. And of those sent to Kauai's Hanamaulu Plantation, we were seven.

I arrived in Hanamaulu on May 1, 1922, and began working on May 3. Because many of my work companions were Japanese, we learned to speak in some kind of an English. If my companions were Filipino, however, I used Filipino. At that time, there were mostly Visayans. There were some Ilocanos, but not very many. Not like now.

Kālai, cutting cane, was my first work. After four or five months at Hanamaulu, I was given a better kind of work. I became a ditchman, a guy who makes sure that the water goes into the irrigation ditch.

The big *luna*, or big boss, had me transferred over to this place near a waterfall. I began to live by the waterfall also, close to the Wailua River. I was supposed to watch over the guys working on the ditches there.

The work was very heavy and we were always being made to go faster by the *luna*. Workers were only being paid ten cents an hour; one dollar per day. I tell you, it was really difficult to work.

This commissioner was sent from the Philippines in order to talk to us and to fix up our situation. His name was Cayetano Ligot, an Ilocano. But, from the time he arrived here, he was already on the side of the plantations. There's no way of knowing whether he received compensation from the plantation owners, but it looked very suspicious. His way of solving the problem was to get Ilocanos to come from the Philippines to replace the dissatisfied workers. That was so the plantation would not have a hard time and be lacking labor.

Pablo Manlapit, a labor organizer, came here to Kauai, and he gave talks, too. Basically, his talk was that we Filipinos have to pull together, be united, and then we can raise our salary. Manlapit was going around the plantations and encouraging people to strike so that they could ask for two dollars per day. His purpose was to help workers get higher salaries to better support our families.

Inside my heart, I felt the same as Manlapit. I wished our salaries could be raised—if the plantation would give it. But there was also this thing that if you didn't join the strike, there were strikers who had bad intentions towards you. The strikers, because of their desire for all Filipinos to join together, were saying that if you don't join, something's going to happen to you.

So that's how it happened that in 1924, the Visayans went out on strike.

We went out on strike in Kapaa around June or August, I think. At first, we lived in the Hee Fat Building. It was divided up into four big rooms. When those of us from the waterfall got there, there were already a lot of people. Upstairs and downstairs, all full.

My companions were all married. I was the only one who was still single. We were upstairs, and they took the married people and put them in one room, one after the other. And I was right in the middle because I wasn't married.

We were a lot of strikers, so we took turns guarding the camp. Every night, there would be four or five of us on duty. You see, the plantation really intended to break the strike, so we suspect they paid off different people to infiltrate the camp in order to make trouble.

Right there at the camp, we had a rice mill. There were a lot of materials, like rice hulls, so we were very careful that there wouldn't be any kind of a fire. We were afraid if the place did burn, they would blame it on us.

I myself was not on duty this one night, but a man, a Filipino, was caught trying to burn the mill. He was imprisoned in one of the rooms at the camp. The other strikers wanted to beat him up. We were three, who were speaking against doing anything to this man. That's why nothing happened to him. We turned him over to the police the next day. I think the police just let him go, because after all, he was probably from the plantation. You have to understand the way it was: the plantations ran the government. The plantations determined everything. And their purpose always was to break our strike.

Another time, a policeman on horseback entered the strike camp. Our short, little guard—I think he was half Moro, half Muslim—took a shot at him. The bullet didn't hit him; it just went through his hat. After that, the policeman ran away. That's all there was to it. It was lucky that nothing else happened.

When we were still in the Hee Fat Building, there had been the fighting and killing in Hanapepe [on September 9, 1924]. People died, both strikers and police. Maybe the plantations ordered the Army [National Guard] to come to the Hee Fat Building after that, I don't know.

But on both sides of the road, right near the building, they had machine guns. The purpose of setting up the guns was so the strikers

Photos of Hanapepe incident aftermath, published in *Honolulu Advertiser*,
September 15, 1924. *Reprinted with permission of the Honolulu Advertiser*

here in Kapaa would not go to Hanapepe. With those guns, nobody
could walk to Hanapepe to help the strikers there. How were we going
to go there anyway, if we didn't have some way of riding there? Hanapepe is very far, and there was no way of walking there.

I felt very sad about what happened in Hanapepe and prayed it
wouldn't happen here in Kapaa because that kind of thing is useless.
It's really very, very difficult if you go up against police who have arms,
and you have next to none.

And we didn't even have money. We couldn't pay anything for living in the building. Later, Hee Fat said, "Hey look, you guys. If you
don't pay rental, then you have to get out." And that's why we moved
to the rear of the building, on the beach.

Everybody was responsible for putting up their own shelter. We
began to make these shacks. To put them up, we found secondhand
lumber, iron roofing, sheet metal, cardboard, anything.

You know, the leaders of the strike appointed me to be a collector to
go around and try to get food for strikers. I would go to whatever plantations we were able to get into and ask for food. For example, Kilauea,
that was a plantation we could get into. And we'd go in there and collect food.

Kauai isn't that big of a place and most Visayans know each other. I
would tell them, "For those of us who are out on strike, these are very

difficult times, and we could use some help." The Visayans gave, but there were other people also, like the Japanese.

Also, in order to stay alive, someone would go fishing. And during those days, there were a lot of fish in the sea. So among the men, almost everybody had something to do; it usually was fishing or going out collecting.

Women would wash, cook, clean, or things like that. Among the women in the strike camp was the younger sister of my wife. My wife's younger sister came here to Hawaii before she did. My wife didn't get here until December of 1924.

CRESENCIA

I had only the one sister here in Hawaii. She was married in the Philippines before she came. Before I left, I told my mother, "Listen, Mother, don't be sad, because as soon as I find my sister, we're all going to return to the Philippines."

My mother said to me, "You're going over to that faraway place, and you're still an unmarried woman. It might be better if you just find yourself a husband before you go."

I said, "Mom, don't worry about me. You can be sure when I come back I'll still be an unmarried woman." But what could I do? My fate caught up with me while I was here in Hawaii.

We were all *sakada,* recruited sugar plantation workers, on the ship. Some were headed for Ewa or Waipahu. In December of 1924, my uncle, his wife, and I were destined for Kealia. You know, at the time of the strike, I went by, riding in the back of a truck. And I saw so many strikers. A large number of them. I pitied them because they were all living in these very poor shacks. When I looked at them, I said to myself, "Mary, Most Holy Virgin, how bitter it must be for those people who have no work."

When we got to the plantation, my uncle asked me if I wanted to work. I said, "I will if there is work."

He said, "Why don't you take in wash?"

That's how my companion and I began to wash clothes. The work was very hard and the salary was very low. For one person, for one month, they would pay you $2.50. That's why I used to cry a lot. I wanted to come so much to Hawaii, and it turns out to be a very bitter kind of place.

My companion's name was Marcella. And she was saying to me, "Maybe it'd be better if we just got married."

I told her to shut up, because it was very tiresome to get married. I said, "If you like, you go ahead. But I'm not going to get married. I'm just going to make a little bit of money here, and then I'm going back to the Philippines."

Soon a relative of mine came to me and said, "You know, it would be better if we go and work in the fields. The money is better there."

So we got a job in the fields. Our job was to take off the dead leaves of the sugar plant and wrap them up in bundles. I found the work very heavy, and finally decided to go to my sister's house in Kapaa, because it would be a lot better there. Besides, it would be such a waste to have come to Hawaii and not to have seen her.

So there I was, coming to Kapaa, carrying with me my mat—the woven mat people sleep on in the Philippines. I was carrying all the things that I owned. I looked like a real country girl. You know, I probably looked like some woman who comes from the mountains in the Philippines. And that's funny because, really, I come from the city. But, I didn't care what they said about me anyway; I was going to come to Kapaa. I said, "I'm not going back to that plantation, no matter what happens."

But my sister was in the strike camp at that time. And people were saying, "If you go into that camp, the police will kill you. Or even worse, you'll be killed by the strikers themselves." Then, Pedro asked for me and tried to get me to come to the camp.

So I was looking at Pedro and saying to myself, "This is not the husband of my sister. He has a different appearance."

And Pedro said, "I was sent here by your sister because she has just given birth."

"Where is my brother-in-law?"

"He's out fishing."

"I'm not going with you," I said, "because I don't even know you. I'm an unmarried woman and for me to go with you, somebody I don't even know, that's a very dangerous thing to do. There's a lot of this *cowboy-cowboy* [abduction of women] kind of stuff going on." So I refused to go with him.

When I was living in the plantation, there was somebody courting me. We couldn't understand one another's language. This man was from Pampanga, the northern part of the Philippines. His name was Abe. I said to him, "You know, it doesn't make any difference if you speak to me even slower. I still don't understand what you're talking about." I was in no hurry to get married, and besides that, I didn't know the customs or character of this man.

One day Abe came to the house where I was ironing clothes. I was all alone in the house and was not about to open the door for him. "What do you want?" I asked him. Of course, I didn't understand what he was saying because he was speaking in his own language. And he didn't understand what I was saying because I was also using my own language. He started to get angry, kicking the locked door. Finally, from his kicking it, the door finally broke, and he started coming in. I grabbed a hold of the iron, and said to myself, "If he comes in here and grabs me, I'm going to hit him with this iron." I began to shout at the top of my lungs, and the woman who owned the boarding house where he was staying came running.

She said, "What's going on?"

I said, "Well, this man, he's bothering me."

She said, "Hey listen, how come you don't pay any attention to him? You know, he's very good and he loves you."

"Maybe so, but I still don't understand what he's talking about."

So finally, I left there and went to my sister who was inside the strike camp. There were lots of people there. That's where I saw my future husband again. I asked my sister, "Who is that man over there?"

She answered, "That's my *kompadre*." Because he was the sponsor at the baptism of her child.

While I was at the camp, this Pampangan, the one who kicked in the door, came looking for me. And Pedro now became interpreter for this Pampangan who was coming to court me.

PEDRO

I became the interpreter because I can speak a little bit of Tagalog. No matter how I interpreted, though, she would not agree to him because she couldn't understand Tagalog and couldn't take an interpreter with her all her life. So I said, "Abe, it's a good thing if you don't come around anymore. I mean, don't be angry about it, but you cannot understand one another, and besides that, we're on strike here. It's better if you don't come around." After that, Abe didn't come around any more. And then the two of us got married.

CRESENCIA

Actually, I said to Pedro, "Let's not get married right away because I'm still new here in Hawaii." He waited for one year until after the strike.

I tell you, the strike was really a bitter kind of time for us. It was pitiful. There were a lot of people in the strike camp. Both men and women, married and unmarried. We—three women—were making rice cakes and selling them inside the camp. Once a week, we would make them. It's what kept us alive, selling the cakes.

And if anybody inside of the strike camp felt any kind of sickness, they would say to me, "Please help me, Ning [Cresencia's nickname]." Like some people were crippled, they had pains. I helped them; I did it by massaging. And they got better.

PEDRO

You know, this wife of mine, there's a very long story about this power that she has from God to heal people. You can't believe the number of people she has been able to help.

CRESENCIA

This thing started when I was only thirteen or fourteen years old. I didn't like to take it on myself because I was still a child, but my parents wanted me to do it. My father said to me, "Ning, I think you have been chosen by the Lord. You can help your own family and help others."

You see, my father was a healer. He was really very skillful. He never went to school like doctors, of course, but he was an excellent doctor.

He would bring different roots and grasses home, wash them off, and clearly label them so that he would have medicines available for any kind of sickness. And the medicines would sometimes be applied to the outside of the body and sometimes, boiled with water and drunk.

When Good Friday would come around, he would say to me, "Ning, we're going to go together."

I said, "Where?"

"We're going up to the cave, up there in the mountains."

I was really scared. "I don't like to go, Dad, because it's really scary. I'm afraid."

He would say, "Don't be afraid. When we get up there, we're going to enter the cave and we won't talk at all." And my father told me, "Don't forget to bring along a candle." He would have five candles in one hand, in the spaces between his fingers, and five in the other.

When I'd go inside that cave, you know, there'd be an awful lot of bats hanging in there. Really dark. But I wouldn't say anything because he told me not to talk.

When we would come out of the cave, on the way home, he would
say to me, "You know, Ning, it's a good thing that you came with me
and not your older sister. Because she talks an awful lot, and that can't
be done in the cave while I'm gathering medicine."

I'd say to him, "Why is it like that?"

He'd say, "That's the will of God. This ability that I have to cure, it's
a gift given to me by God for other people."

There was a time, maybe around 1912, when there was an epidemic
in our place in the Philippines, around Cebu. Whatever it is that leaves
these little scars all over your face. Diphtheria or smallpox. There were
neighbors on both sides of us who were laid flat by the sickness and
died.

During this epidemic, my father burned weeds or grasses that caused
a lot of smoke. The smell was very sweet, very nice smelling. He said,
"It's a medicine against the epidemic." We were five brothers and
sisters in our family and no one got sick.

When everything subsided, people would come around and ask my
father—his name was Sebastian—"*Manong* Sebastian, why is it that no
one in your house gets sick?"

My father would just answer, "You know, by the mercy of God, no
one in our house got sick. Our prayers were heard."

He was a deeply religious man. He would go to church every day.

One Sunday, after receiving the Holy Communion at the altar rail, I
came back to my seat. I looked, and my father didn't come back. He
didn't stand up after receiving Communion. And so I went up there to
get him. The priest came down and said, "Your father has died."

I was hugging my father and beginning to cry. The priest said to me,
"Don't cry, because your father's death is a very beautiful one. His
spirit has gone to God."

My father had said that, like him, I had been chosen by the Lord to
help people. When I was fourteen years old, there were people coming
to the house—men and women—asking that I give them a massage. I
was really embarrassed because I was fourteen years old and there were
people asking for this.

I said to my mother, "Why are those people here?"

One woman, who had just been married, said, "I've come here
because my stomach is painful."

You know, at that time in the Philippines, out in the rural areas,
there were no doctors. My mother would say, "You know, it's a good
thing if you give a massage to this woman."

So I massaged her. While I was giving her a massage, I realized she was conceiving. I said to her, "You know why you're feeling pain in your stomach? It's because you're pregnant."

She said, "Is that the way it is? Are you sure?"

I said, "Yeah, really. You wait about five months after I finish massaging you this time. Then come back here and I'll check you again."

That's how I began being a *hilot*—massager's not a good word for it, but sort of like a folk doctor—up until now.

PEDRO

Even women who want to have children and can't conceive, she's able to help them also. After how many months, they become pregnant. Or, for example, if somebody gets a sprain or gets crippled, she's able to help them. Once there was a horse that was crippled. By massaging it, she was able to get the horse running again. From the time in the strike camp up until the present time, I am quite surprised at the power she has to help people in the way of healing.

CRESENCIA

But the time of the strike was really bitter. We in the strike camp really had a big hope that we would win. But it was really hard. There was a lot of trouble that came from the plantations. Even the women were helping, watching and guarding. If I had known ahead of time that it was like this, I don't think I would have come to the camp.

PEDRO

When I look back on the strike . . . you know, we were asking for two dollars for one day, and we just couldn't get it. We tried our best, but they wouldn't agree to it. It seems like it was not successful. But, thank God, nothing like what happened in Hanapepe happened here.

The strike was broken here in Kapaa when we were rounded up by government police in the wee hours one morning [May 16, 1925]. At that time, we were asleep in our small houses on the beach. It was the guns that woke us up. Then they started shouting at us, "Okay, okay, get up, get up."

I asked them, "Why is it that you hold guns to our heads when we haven't done anything wrong?"

They told us to get up and change. They brought along a big truck. It was hard to fight back because we were taken inside of the truck. They left the women behind and took the men. It didn't make any difference if we were married or single, as long as we were men, they took us along.

There was a Japanese *luna,* Sakaguchi, for whom I had worked. The very next day, he got me out of jail. That's why I only spent one night in jail, while my companions were there a long time. They didn't want to give up, and, of course, there was no place for them to work anyway. They were probably thinking to themselves, "Well, it's just as well to be here in jail because at least there's something to eat."

When they got out of jail, some of my companions went back to work in the sugar plantation. Some went to work in pineapple. Others even went to America, to the Mainland, to work there. And some went home by themselves to the Philippines.

I didn't want to go back to the plantation any more because of the bitterness I encountered. It's a hard life working on the plantation. The long hours that you work, the little pay. So it was lucky that I had done some barbering in the Philippines. After the strike, I opened a barbershop in Kapaa. And in 1925, me and my wife, we decided that we would marry each other.

CRESENCIA

After the strike, I was working in the cannery. Then my fellow workers in the cannery came up to me and said, "There're three guys downstairs who are looking for you." They were very excited because the three who were looking for me looked like *cowboys.* Girls were very much afraid, at that time, of being *cowboyed.* The three men were cousins of Pedro. They were really anxious that Pedro and I get married and not wait too long. So I finally said to myself, "Maybe I should just agree to what Pedro is asking." Because he loved me, and I loved him, too. So when I agreed, we got married.

And today, I really have to thank God for all the difficult things we've gone through, because by the grace of God, we're still alive. We were able to arrive at the time and place we're at now.

Emigdio Cabico
LUCKY I NEVER WORK FIELD

Emigdio Cabico was born August 9, 1909, in Pangasinan, Philippines. At the age of seventeen, he immigrated to Hawaii. Since Emigdio was below the age of immigration at the time, he came to the islands under his older brother's name and papers. Despite having only a fifth-grade education, Emigdio impressed Waialua Sugar Plantation officials with his ability to speak and write English. This skill enabled him to work as a clerk in a Waialua plantation store. Because Filipino immigrants were often given the most menial jobs in the sugar cane fields, Emigdio felt fortunate to work under more favorable conditions.

Emigdio's ability to communicate effectively—in English or in pidgin —with the different ethnic groups helped him achieve a measure of success in business. This was no easy task, since conflicts between and among ethnic groups were common. There were frequent confrontations between Visayans and Ilocanos, speakers of the two main Filipino dialects used in Hawaii. Although Visayans, who came from the Visayan Islands arrived in large numbers prior to 1925, from 1919, Filipino immigrants increasingly came from the northern part of Luzon, known as the Ilocos provinces. The Visayans and Ilocanos came to Hawaii with different languages, cultures, and values. These differences coupled with the presence of *haoles*, Portuguese, Japanese, and others living and working in the area made adjustment to plantation life difficult.

In 1936, Emigdio was promoted from clerk to manager. In 1948, he utilized the expertise and clientele gained as manager to start his own store in the neighboring town of Haleiwa.

He gave up the business in 1956, and worked as a school custodian,

restaurant clerk, cashier, and cook. Now retired, Emigdio lives in Waialua.

Emigdio was interviewed in 1976, as part of an ESOHP oral history
project focused on plantation life. Pablo Lazo, then a University of
Hawaii student and Waialua resident, conducted interviews in Emigdio's home. Just after meeting Emigdio for the first time, Pablo recorded his impressions about the man and the surroundings: "He did
not look a bit like a sixty-seven-year-old; he looked fresh, and healthy. I
don't think he ever wears a shirt in the house. . . . I think that he is
more than willing to share his experiences with us. He is glad we're doing this sort of project—to know about life in the old days."

In terms of status and independence, Emigdio achieved a higher
degree of success than many of his compatriots—while he worked as a
store clerk, others toiled in the canefields; while he managed his own
business, most Filipinos remained at the lower rungs of Hawaii's socio-
economic ladder. Despite these contrasts, Emigdio throughout his life
empathized with working people and never forgot how fortunate he was
to have never worked in the fields.

THERE IS ONE AGENT, sent by the Hawaiian Sugar Planters' Association
[H.S.P.A.], to recruit labor for Hawaii. He explain to us about Hawaii.
He says it's good to come. The agent promise us if we stay here for three
years, we have free passage to go back home. Then if we wanted to come
back again, all us can come back to Hawaii free passage. See, free.
Yeah, that's what they promise us. Of course, when we reach Hawaii,
he said we would have free house and everything, you know. And, the
work contract is eighteen dollars a month. So, naturally, we, young
boys, was listening him one time. We told him we are interested to
come to Hawaii. I wanted to come to continue my studies and earn
money, particularly to help my parents.

But, he said he will recruit only those person the age of twenty-one or
twenty-two. I was only sixteen—I was underage. Besides that, there's
lots of red tape. I have to go get permit from my parent and go to the
municipal mayor to sign, but this, I never did. So, I just borrow my
brother's personal tax paper as proof of being twenty-one. I went to the
H.S.P.A. office at Manila. They don't know me anyway. I said, "I am
Severino. Here's my personal tax. I'm at the age of twenty-one." So
they took me. I used the name of my brother. Otherwise, I cannot
come, you see. That's the only way I could come.

I arrived here in Hawaii, that was January 1926. About sixty-five people arrived here in Waialua; most of us does not know how to speak English and write. Naturally, the clerks, especially *haole,* could hardly spell our names. So, they ask us who can write and spell. Since I attended up to three months in the fifth grade, I raise my hand. I write all the names, and when they see that my handwriting is so nice, they thought I'm a well-educated man. That's what happened. (Laughs) Then they assign us to Kawailoa, but they told me don't work on that day, because they wanted to talk to me.

So, that morning, I didn't show up to work and the policeman came to my house and told me, "Eh, boy, you going jail!"

I say, "Why?"

"You go in the plantation office because the manager want to see you."

I say, "Oh, okay." We went to the office and the manager ask me what kind of job I wanted. I said, "I'm not so choosy. Any kind."

"Do you want to work in the hospital? Work in the office? Or work in the store?"

"Well, I prefer to work in the store, if you give me a chance."

He said, "Well, you take the test. If you pass the test, then you are qualified to work in the store."

So that day, we are about eight to take the test. They give us pencil, tablet; all the test was written in the blackboard. Within thirty or thirty-five minute, I would say, I finish. It was so simple.

Of course, I can write good, so I make it fancy. When I finished, the examiner said, "Cabico, you cannot write this way if you only low grade in the Philippine. Must be you graduate in Santo Tomas University." (Laughs)

I say, "No, sir. I'm not."

Then the policemen trying to scare me. They said, "If you don't tell the truth, you going jail."

I was new then and kind of scared. "Why I didn't—I'm telling the truth." But they wouldn't believe me; they still tell me go in jail. So I went to see the manager and told him, "Sir, is that right? You put me in jail? For not telling the truth?"

He said, "No, they only kidding you."

So, from the next day, they took me to the plantation store. That's how I get my job as a clerk.

From the beginning I work in the store so I didn't work hard. But others work in the field, eh, and whenever they come home from work, I see them. They are so tired; their job is so hard. Maybe, I'm very fortunate that I never work in the field.

But, one thing, the hours at the store were even more long than the hours in the field. We open the store four o'clock, early in the morning. You see, the man taking charge trying to make good to the plantation so he open early. Then, in the afternoon, we go home five o'clock, take a bath, eat supper; and go back again to the store, six o'clock. And we close again at eight o'clock p.m. And . . . mind you, one dollar one day. That's all we are getting. One dollar one day.

As a clerk my duty is to sell to our countrymen, in fact, to everybody. But, when I went to the store, there were five stock clerks and they were Visayan. Because I am Ilocano, they don't like me very much. They don't even care to talk with me so how can I learn the prices? Especially since they don't mark the price on the item. So, I ask one of them, "Why don't you teach me?"

He say, "It's up to you to learn."

I say, "Oh, okay, that's how you feel."

Then I went to the one taking charge. They call him branch manager. I said, "My goodness, how do I know? How you expect me to sell the goods, if you don't put the price?" All the prices, he tell me. But he don't write. So whenever he tell me, I put it down. In three months, gradually, I know all the prices—every item inside the store.

Then the problem, again. Since I'm the only Ilocano working in the store, most all the Ilocano customers come to me. They don't go to the Visayan clerks, because the Visayans speak to them Visayan or English. They cannot understand one another. So, I told the clerks, "Please don't talk Visayan to them; after all, they are not Visayan. Why don't you talk Tagalog to them? Probably some of them can understand Tagalog." But still, the Visayans don't do that; they talk English to them. Majority of Ilocanos cannot understand English. They just arrive from the Philippine Islands and didn't even learn how to speak pidgin English. So I get hard time.

After three or four month, I wrote a note to the general manager that I get hard time in the store. Then he came up and ask me why. "Because these clerks here don't work. How can you expect me to serve more than 200 people every day? Only myself serving them. The other clerks don't even help me."

He said, "Why?"

"Because, mostly all our customers Ilocano, and the clerks speak Visayan to them, and they don't understand Visayan. And the Ilocano speak Ilocano to the clerks who don't understand Ilocano. So naturally they all come to me. And even I ask help, at least, when I pick up the good, at least the clerks put in the bag, uh? But they didn't do that."

They fired two guys on account of doing like that. Then, also, the truck driver that used to go around and deliver goods. He's fired.

The boss ask me again. "Do you recommend somebody?"

"Yes. I want the Ilocano to come in." So the two Ilocano (chuckles) came in. That's the time, I feel good already, because, after all, we are all three Ilocano. So when those Ilocano come, we can serve the customers very well, because we are already three. And, get three more left. Visayan. So, they only serve the Visayan people. But, like me, seems I easily learn their language. I can speak Visayan. So whenever they come I can serve them also.

When I work in the store, I learn quick. In fact, I learn most all the language in the camp. Like, Japanese. All the simple word, Japanese, Puerto Rico, and Portuguese. Whenever they come, well, I cannot speak very well, but, at least, I understand. We understand each other by talking in pidgin Japanee or pidgin Puerto Rican. That's why we have good service.

Eventually, I earn and save a little. After six month I worked here, I send money to my parents to make them feel happy. I send them $100 and with that money, they bought land. Four hectare. They clear the place and plant any kind of vegetable. That's how they live, happy; they don't have a hard life like it used to be. Then the following six month, I send them again, and they did the same thing. They do not have to be a tenant anymore. They worked for our land; they was so happy that I came to Hawaii.

And me, well, I just continue to work. When I arrived in the plantation, there is no recreation at all—not much people yet. People start coming in about '28, '29, '30, '31, '32. Since everybody's young, seventeen, eighteen, twenty, twenty-one, we like to play. We organize ourself. In each camp, we have a baseball team. Every Sunday, in the baseball park—big crowd. We challenge each camp. I do the score. I do the planning and everything—scheduling which team going play. In that camp, Kawailoa, our team was champion. But we challenge different camp, we lose. (Laughs) Well, that's the game. We don't expect to win all the time. Sometime we lose.

Then we buy five cases of soda water. Or ten cases soda water. (Laughs) And doughnut. Ten dozen! Whatever we agreed. After the game, everybody full, eh, because they get doughnut, pastry, and drink, see. But no liquor, only soda water. Some, they make homemade brew (laughs). We cannot buy liquor before. So that's what we did.

Sometime, of course, those who wanted to play volleyball make their own team. See? So, Saturday night, we challenge each camp. In each camp, we have volleyball. The best player was in Helemano Camp. They really play good volleyball. Nobody can beat them. Then, I make an arrangement that they could play any other plantation. So, I took them over to Waipahu, Ewa. They smart. Again, nobody beat them. They really too good.

Baseball, volleyball—that's the only recreation we had before. And, of course, the plantation was so kind enough that they make clubhouse in the camp. Theaters, like that. So, we have a movie once a week. We pay only ten cents. Later on, they make a big gym. After that, they make a swimming pool. Then, a tennis court. Some of the young boys learn any kind of sport. Any kind. So we have good fun in the camp.

And every year, when we have holiday, specially Rizal Day, we celebrate. Oh! We have big program in the camp. We donated seventy-five cents, each guy. With that money, we could buy pig, we could buy cow. So Saturday night, we make a blowout. We invited all the plantation bosses, all different race in the camp. And they like the celebration because they like eat Filipino food, eh. We had a smart cook and he can cook about fifteen different kind of food. All the *haole* really like to eat and they surprise because so many kind of food. So, every year, we have a big occasion. Plenty people. We invite all, even a friend who live someplace. Free. We don't charge.

In the camp, there are some boys that really have a talent. They know how to play music. Some play saxophone, some play *bandorya,* violin, or guitar. We don't pay any single cent, but we had to feed them, see. That's their payment, just to feed them. That's what we used to do. No problem in those days. And, we have a social dance sometime once or twice a month. We make blowout to feed the girls and the parent. So just like picnic, then we dance.

In fact, I meet my first wife during the social dance. You had to find your own partner in order to dance. So that's what I did. I found she's townmate and full Pangasinan. Although she was born here in Hawaii, she know how to speak Tagalog, Pangasinan and Ilocano. So that's the beginning. I court her and it happen that we love each other so we get married. And 1931, we have one son. Then, you know how it is. After 1932, she take off, leave the baby. Since I'm working, I cannot care, so, I let my friend take care for me. See, I pay fifteen dollars a month to take care my baby. Then when the boy grow up little bit, I took him to the real mother, because she willing to take care. Then when he go to school, the boy came back again to me. At the time, he's big already and I don't have to hire somebody to take care my son.

By that time, by working honestly, they put me as Kawailoa branch store manager. The other guy who used to be a manager did something wrong, and that moment, they ask me, and I told the truth. So they fired him out and put me as manager. I'm the head in the store for total over ten years, 1936 to 1948.

And those years, I had to be very careful. If you, a worker, goes to a store outside the plantation you have to pay cash. You cannot buy without cash. They don't trust you to keep your credit, especially if they don't know you. But, in the plantation store you don't have to pay cash, they call that charge or credit. But . . . after the end of the month, payday, they will deduct from your pay, whatever you owe to the store. And, the order that workers can only have a particular credit amount is from the plantation manager, and the general manager of the plantation stores gives a report to the manager of the plantation. If one store gives out too much credit, then, the manager of that store will get scolding for that.

Why, we even have scolding or maybe get fired or something like that, when the cash register tape and money doesn't balance. Every afternoon, when I close the store, I take out the tape. I figure how much the money and it balance. Sometimes it doesn't balance. Sometime, short. If five cents short, I have to cover up. We have also a gasoline pump in the store. Before, I know what time, what day the auditor come. So I check up and if two gallon short, I put under my *bangō,* so that when the auditor come, well, exact. But when I read in the magazine that gasoline evaporate, then I came smart.

When the auditor come, he say, "Cabico, you short two, five gallons of gasoline."

I say, "Well, short, that's it. Evaporate, the gasoline. Didn't you know that, sir?"

He say, "No."

"Yes, sir." Well, I fight them, then they report to the plantation manager that Cabico is short five gallon.

So, he called me up. He said, "Cabico, you were right. You fight for your right. The gasoline evaporate, you know. So you don't have to pay anything. If short, short."

So I feel good, because the plantation manager back me up. Before, I don't know; I have to pay because I don't want to get scolding from the auditor.

And, every day on every item in the store I have to put the cost price and the selling price. So when inventory, the bookkeeper easy to figure the profit and the loss. I had to be very careful, because if I know the selling price and don't know the cost, going be hard time—scolding from the general manager. So have to be very careful on that.

And, I make sure we have good service in the store and sell our goods. Like the ingredients and container for home-brew. You see? These things, I had to introduce to my customer, because after all, I have to make money, eh. I sell them the container, I sell them the hop, I sell them the yeast cake. Anyway, each cake is only five cent before. But the hops is seventy-five cents one can, you see. And the container, two dollar half. See. I show them so that they know how to make their own brew. (Laughs) Then, I can sell more container, because the more I sell, the more I make money. Same thing with typewriter. Me, I don't know how to type. Yet when I put all my fingers on the keys, I know all the letters. So I show them how to type. That's how I sold plenty typewriter.

Those days, those who knows how to save like me, well, we save money. But those who only wanted to go around, those are people that no more money. (Laughs) Plenty Filipinos broke their money by buying new car. Sometime, five of them, together, buy car. And if one quit paying and they cannot carry the payment, the garage take back the car. So that's why they cannot save money. In fact, they lose money.

Me, I bought my own car in 1939. I can go to town. I can make money, so I don't have to worry about the car payment. I take passengers to town, Honolulu side.

When we were new in the camp, hardly don't know nothing about Honolulu. But, there is a Japanese man—he's really good to the Filipino. So, he come to me, "Cabico, you tell your countrymen that if they wanted to go Honolulu, I have three cars available." And he said, "I can take them around if they want to go Honolulu." Naturally, those Filipinos and even myself wanted to go Honolulu, because I didn't see Honolulu. Go, come back, the charge only fifty cents. Mostly every Saturday night, oh, sometime, two time, three cars.

So the Japanese man taught us to go to the hotel. That's in Nuuanu. Now, no more that building. They call Nuuanu and Hotel. And someplace near Aala Park. There are two kind. If you go to the "white meat," they charge five dollars, one pound. If you go to the "mix," you can buy even two dollar, one pound. But since they go to the ordinary one, or "mix," some get sick. So, they go to the doctor and he advise them don't go that place any more. So, everybody go to the white meat in the hotel. Five dollar. So, I learn all those places and how to go in town. Then I bought my own car.

Whenever I take passenger and take to the place, hotel, the one who is taking charge the house give me one dollar each. I bring five men, they give me five dollar. So, I make money, I can afford to pay my monthly payment on my car. Every Sunday, sometime I go Saturday night, Sunday night. Sometime during the day, two time, two trip, because I say, "Eh, you like meat? White meat?"

They say, "Sure! Why not?"

I charge them only fifty cents just to go and come back. But in Honolulu, the hotel give me one dollar each. I make more money (laughs) I don't care, eh. Even if the men don't pay me, the hotel pay me. So, naturally, I save my money. I can afford to pay my car payment every month, because I can make money. Saturday and Sunday, like that. Sometime even weekdays. Especially after payday, we go Honolulu. But, we have to go to the white meat, five dollar. You know what I mean? (Laughs) You see.

After that, those girl found out . . . I think, somebody—I don't know, maybe Filipino—invite them to come in the camp. So, they contact me in the store, because that's the only telephone.

"Will you tell those people that we are coming?"

And I said, "All right. What day?" So they ask me what day the payday. I said, "Oh, certain day, payday."

"So, we come that night."

I say, "Okay."

So, I have to notify all in the camp that somebody is coming. The women come and charge $2.50, one pound. Only $2.50 is cheap. But, no more white meat. (Laughs) If $2.50, they make two dollar, because they give me fifty cents.

Then, I read in the newspaper that it's not allowed to do that. Be in trouble if you get caught. I entirely quit, especially, since I'm store manager. If plantation find out that I'm soliciting people, I'm in trouble. (Laughs) So, I told in the camp, "From now on I don't any more solicit you folks. So it's up to you guys now. If you get caught, that's too bad." So that's what they been doing all the time until today. But I'm not soliciting any more, because I don't want to be involved. (Laughs) If you get caught, you be in trouble. So, like before, well, we don't know about the law. Even in Honolulu, is open. No more policeman or anybody else coming around. Maybe they are not so strict before. Although, maybe, that's already against the law, but not so strict.

Yeah, those days I can make money. Gasoline so cheap, so plenty. Only during World War II, we cannot go around so much, because with the ten-gallon ration, my goodness. You go to town only one time (laughs). So, hardly nobody go to town because gasoline ration.

Also the liquor. You cannot buy liquor unless you have a permit. They allow you only to buy one quart of whiskey a week. Those who drink, well, they had to have permit. Those who don't drink, well, (chuckles) you don't have to bother about permit.

You know, I remember the wartime, especially Pearl Harbor day (December 7, 1941). That was Sunday morning. I was giving gasoline to my customer, we saw airplane that almost touch the cane field. We were surprised and we was talking, "Gee, how come this airplane so low?" The first time we see an airplane flying low. Then, after three minutes, I guess, or two minutes, we heard machine gun, in the camp—Brodie 4. And not more than one or two minute later, we heard the big explosion, just like one thunder. That was in Wheeler Field. They bomb the airplane and the warehouse, but we don't know what is going on. When people in the store went home and open their radio, that's the time they find out that it's war.

After so many hours, we heard all the big trucks passing down the road. All the big cannon and all the traffic. We cannot go out so much, because all the big truck and all the cannon go around by the beach. In fact, every place. All the munitions in Schofield, I think, came out.

After a week everybody was notified about blackout in the house. You cannot use your light. So, you come home early. You cook early. Every night, there's some guard going around here and if they see light, they knock the door and say, "Your light is on." So very, very strict those days. And after a week everybody had to build their bomb shelter. Every house, had to make their bomb shelter. So, we make.

After two months, the Army come around telling us that not only them going fight the enemy, but us civilian going fight, too. So, naturally, they teach us how to use the gun and cannon, machine gun and all whatnot. So, in each camp, like the camp where I was, we have a drill every afternoon. They call us Home Guard. We all happy, because we know how to march and how to hold the gun. We enjoy that.

As far as I'm concerned, the only one I'm afraid, before, that Filipinos get mad. Especially when they heard news that the Japanese soldiers so cruel to the Filipino family in the Philippine. That's the one we are afraid.

They said, "Oh God! My goodness, they kill my mother! They kill my brother! So I going kill some of the Japanese here, too."

Say, "No, no, you don't do that! Because we are here in America! If you do that, you are going to be killed yourself, too. They put you in jail. If you kill somebody, they put you in jails your entire life! So don't do that."

Strikers at Kawailoa Plantation Store, 1946. *Courtesy ILWU*

Then, afterward, they cool off. They don't bother. As usual, all the Japanese very friendly, the old folks included. We talk as usual. No hard feeling. We all work together.

And, sometime the plantation tell the workers to go that Army side and work, see. The workers get paid the same plantation pay. So, I think they have a connection between the plantation and the Army. If the Army want some place cleared they could tell the plantation. Then the plantation will tell the workers. During the war, plenty went out from the plantation because they rather work in the defense job. They get more pay than in the plantation. Some came back because the plantation convinced them to come back. But, some never come back even after the war.

After the war, I think in 1946, the plantation strike. Everybody don't work. But, I cannot join the union because I was store manager. I wanted to join with them, but the union leaders said, " No, you cannot join with us, because we cannot fight for you. So better for you to stay out." They picket the store so that nobody allowed to go inside the store. Only myself can go in. But, good fun (laughs) because when they need cigarette, they need sugar, they need coffee, they call me from the back window. We make that way. Secret way. Anything they buy, it's from the back window. Not from the door. (Laughs)

The plantation said that since the strikers make a picket line in front the store, don't sell to any of them. I say, "Okay. I take the order." But in secret, outside, I sell from the window. Because I pity them. Where they going buy? (Laughs) They no more coffee, they no more sugar, or soap for take a bath, anything. So, what they need, they know where to go. By the back window. (Laughs)

I remember, later, they set the soup kitchen. All the union leader appoint a cook. They appoint some to go fishing early in the morning. They appoint someone to plant vegetable for them. So they did that. Is good. Is real good. When they caught plenty fish, sometime they give me. From the window. (Laughs) Because I'm good to them, eh. That's how I remember the strike.

And, after the strike, oh, boy, the *luna* really good. Friendly, laughing, joking. I know, because the workers tell me the story when they come home from work. "Eh, what today?"

"Very good. No more calling us bad names. No more '*bayaw*,' no more '*manong*,' no more '*salalabit*,' no more '*bagoong*'! They all good. Everybody's good."

As long as you work and don't sleep on your job, you don't have to hustle up like it used to be. Maybe, the union go after the *luna* if you make a big noise. They will report to the management. I didn't work in the field, but that's how the workers told me. Whenever they come to the store, they tell me, "Eh, everything good. Now days. No such thing as yelling at us." Everybody feel good. (Laughs)

The union won the strike so they get raise and better working condition. Of course, the plantation said, "Well, since you're making so much now, you have to pay for the water. You have to pay for the house." So that's what they did. But the workers don't care because they get high pay. They can afford to pay because the price very reasonable. Some house rent is eighteen dollars. Some is twenty dollar. And water, they pay only one dollar a month. It's still cheap. It's better than working long hours and you getting free firewood and kerosene. It's better to work short hours and high pay, you don't mind to pay the house rent or water every month. And, after the union, the price at the store is the same. No cut, no raise. Well, only gradually, every year, the price goes up. So, we had to follow other stores' prices.

Anyway, I stayed at the Kawailoa store only until 1948. Before I quit, I have to prepare myself. I bought a property at Haleiwa. I bought one lot, almost one acre. It cost me only thirty-seven cents square foot. So cheap. So first I built my store, I call all my friend to come help me build it. We didn't hire contractor. After I build the store, I hired contractor to build my house. When my house was ready, I told the plantation I will resign. I resign.

I had a small capital, and of course, I knew all the people in the camp and what they want, so I open my store. I used to go around the camp and whatever they need, I always can get from the wholesaler. I don't stock so much in my own store, but I have all the catalog from the wholesaler. So I show them the catalog and if they want, I order today; tomorrow, it come. All the camps. They make money, so they buy more watches, newer radio, big radio, things like that. That's how I make business. And I have a liquor store. All the people drinking, especially in the camp. I supply them beer and they come to me because I have no overhead. Only me and my family with the second wife run the store. I can make competition, I make money. I only didn't watch my credit carefully. I'm not so good, I think, in business. I get soft-hearted. I extend too much credit. If I'm strict, maybe I am something today. The first three, four years in the store, I make good money. But, as I said, I didn't watch out.

Besides that, I was one of the victim. For being greedy, that's what been happen to me. Somebody fleece me during the 1949 stevedore strike. Not only me, but I am the most affected. Some Haleiwa businessmen, Japanese, were fleeced, too.

One salesman came to me and ask me, "Cabico, you need rice?"

"Yes." Well, I knew that salesman because he used to work for the wholesaler. He ask me how many bag of rice. I said, "As much as you can. How much you can get me?"

He said, "I have one boat coming. And that boat will get about 10,000 bag of rice. Ten thousand bag. How many bag you want? You want 5,000 bag?"

"Sure."

When I ordered that rice, I give him about twenty dollars a bag. That's twenty dollars for 100-pound bag. I was thinking if they deliver that rice and I can sell thirty-five or thirty dollars a bag black market, I make money. All right. Plenty guys order five bag, three bag, you know. The first week, twenty-five bags come in from the wholesaler.

But, what happen? The rest of the rice never come. The salesman, *haole* man, never come, never show up. So my money's gone. That's what been happen, I went sunk. All what I have, all my money gone. Beside that, I extend too much credit. People don't pay me regularly, so naturally I cannot keep up any more. That's how I came . . . little bit fall down that time.

I think almost ten years I have my store. I really don't have the capital already so naturally I cannot get supply. I had to look around for a job. Then, when I get the job, still my pay is so small I cannot afford the store any more. So I sold my place. I sold it in 1956.

Then, see, I work as custodian at Waialua High School. And then, when I come home, I take bath. Then I go to Kemoo Farm as a clerk and cashier. Fifteen years I work there. Believe it or not. I work all around. I work in the Kemoo Farm store until eight o'clock. Then, after eight o'clock, they put me in the kitchen as a fry cook. I'm not very particular. I like learn how to cook. Sometime they put me in the bar to be a bartender. I am very interested. I learn. Sometime they put me in the bakery. Custard pie, pumpkin pie, I learn how to bake those things. Then, sometime they put me in a cashier in the dining room. See, that's how I make my experience, by meeting so many people. Especially soldier. When payday—mind you, all line up in the store to buy liquor, like that, see. By mingle with other people, that's how I improve my social standing. By mingle with the racial group. I can get along with people. I like to meet people. Especially when I was working in the Kemoo Farm store. Because, of course, when they come to the store, you have to be nice to them, and very courteous and, they like you that way. Suppose to be that way. That's why I have good name with Kemoo Farm because I know how to deal with people. I have no trouble at all. Not like the other guy, they have trouble with customer. So far, me, no. Fifteen years I worked there. No trouble.

I been retired now and since I live here all my life, I think Haleiwa-Waialua is the best for me and especially my children. When they were young, they like it so much over here because near the beach and have plenty park. They can play. We had gymnasium and everything is good. When they grown up, they had to seek a better place to live, and, so, most of my children on the Mainland. In fact, most all in the service until today. My oldest son is a full colonel, now. He came here last year and told me, "One more promotion, daddy. I'll be brigadier general so you be proud. I will be the first Filipino brigadier general." So I wish him luck in his work.

And, me, thanks to God, . . . I'm healthy, and I hope it will continue so that I'll be able to maybe someday go back to the Philippines and make my residence. But in the meantime, only me and my third wife and the adopted children will stay in Haleiwa-Waialua. Now, the boy is going to be eleven years old and the girl's going to be ten. And there's a law, eh, if adopted children, they have to be here Hawaii two years, then they can qualify to acquire citizenship. I already apply for their American citizenship, so by next month, they are American. We all American citizen.

IV
In the Small Town

Violet Hew Zane
BORN IN THE STORE

ESOHP

Her father, Hew Fat, started the family business in 1906, after arriving in Lower Paia, Maui from Pukut Village, China. Violet was born soon after, in 1909, and began working in Hew's Store and Restaurant at a very young age. The second of nine children, she also helped her parents take care of her younger brothers and sisters. Much of her early years were spent working as dishwasher, waitress, store clerk, bookkeeper and babysitter.

In 1927, Violet left Lower Paia to attend the University of Hawaii in Honolulu, returning to Maui during her summer vacations to help in the store. In 1931, she married an airline pilot and lived in China between 1934 and 1936. In 1936, she returned to Lower Paia and subsequently became a teacher.

Three years later, she again left Maui to attend the University, this time for a Master's degree in education. From 1941 until her retirement in 1971, she was an elementary school teacher on Maui. Even with a full-time career, Violet was always involved with the store and restaurant.

A longtime resident of this rural community in Central Maui, Violet has been a keen observer of the many historical and social changes that took place around her. Lower Paia, like many other small towns adjacent to sugar plantations, was a social and commercial center for plantation laborers living in scattered camps.

Chinese, who made up a large part of the immigrant plantation labor force during the late nineteenth and early twentieth centuries, lived in camps of the Maui Agricultural Company within walking distance of Lower Paia. They, along with independent farmers in outlying rural areas, made up a large part of Hew Fat's clientele.

However, as more lucrative and independent work opportunities arose elsewhere, most of the Chinese plantation laborers and farmers left the area during the early twentieth century. Japanese, who became the dominant ethnic group on the plantation, took over businesses run formerly by Chinese.

Hew Fat, despite the changing social conditions in Lower Paia, remained in business. Today, with the sugar industry decline and residents moving to the modern city of Kahului, Hew's Store and Restaurant stands alone among boarded-up storefronts and curio shops run mainly by young *haole* newcomers.

Amidst this contrasting setting of old against new, Violet Zane sat in her home behind Hew's Store and Restaurant with interviewer Warren Nishimoto and recalled the origins, daily operation, and survival of the family business. "You have to keep asking me questions. That's the only way I'll remember," the gray-haired, seventy-one-year-old Chinese woman reminded her visitor. She proceeded to recall the social activities of the many Chinese living in or near the once-lively town, and the customs and beliefs the Chinese brought with them from the old country.

Her story, however, focuses on her pride in her parents' accomplishments, her own tireless involvement, and the success of the family business.

I'VE SEEN PAIA CHANGE quite a bit. Originally, there were a lot of Chinese living here—working on the plantation and operating businesses. From the time my parents started the Hew Store and Restaurant in 1906, I would say three-fourths of Paia's businesses were Chinese. Then, around 1920, the Chinese people started to move out. They never came back after they left Maui. Some followed their children to Honolulu or to the Mainland. A few went back to China. And, oh, lots of them are dead now. If you visit the Chinese cemetery, you'll find many dead Chinese. Today, there are only three families of Chinese left here. Our family, the Chee family, and the Wong family.

If you walk up the street and down, you'll find many businesses run by Caucasians from the Mainland. Actually, if it weren't for them, Paia would be a ghost town. Just a few stores run by local people are left here now.

Our store and restaurant is still here, run by my sister-in-law. My parents were considered successful in business. Even when there were hardly any Chinese in Paia, they wouldn't give up a good business like that to go elsewhere, like Honolulu, and take a chance at a new location.

I was born and raised in the store, and I worked there most of my life. I was the second in the family. My oldest sister didn't know much about the business because she was away to boarding school most of the early years. The others were too young, and they didn't spend as much time in the store and restaurant as I did. I knew more about it than anybody else in the family.

My parents really worked hard—getting up early every morning, making bread, pastries, *saimin* noodles. My sister-in-law today doesn't know how to make *saimin* noodles, so she buys the factory-made kind. But she makes the broth somewhat the way we made it, only ours was a little better. You had *saimin* there today? Of course, it would be better if you had our homemade one in the early days.

My parents came to Hawaii from China in 1894. My father was born and raised in Pukut Village, about halfway between Hong Kong and Canton, and my mother was born in the village of Hachoong. That was also halfway between Canton and Hong Kong. Although their families had plenty of land and raised lots of crops, they thought it was easier to make money in Hawaii. My father told me that his foster sister was married to the owner of a restaurant here in Paia, Fung Pao. She told my father to come to Hawaii with her since he had a Chinese education and could take care of Chinese books. So, he came to be their bookkeeper. He was never a laborer.

In 1906, my parents started their own business with $100. They made their own tables and chairs out of wooden boxes. In fact, they made a lot of things by hand. And they started with a three-burner kerosene stove and an oven.

Then the babies started arriving. A midwife brought me into the world on January 24, 1909 in the back section of the store. My mother fed us breast milk—the first eight children. The last one, she worked so hard that she didn't get enough breast milk. Since my brother's stomach ran when he drank fresh milk, my mother fed him canned milk. But, you know, of all the nine children, he was the coldest. Not warm-hearted. And he was the one who died first. So, I was thinking, maybe breast-fed children are healthier than canned milk babies.

My mother strapped us on her back and went to work. That's why she was able to take care of children and work at the same time. And then, when we were old enough, we walked around in the store and restaurant.

We sort of took care of ourselves as soon as we were able to. The older ones would take care the younger ones. So, after my mother got up at 1:30 in the morning to make the bread and all that, she would go to my bed, shake me up, and tell me to feed my brothers. That's how we managed. We understood that my parents were working hard.

As we grew old enough, each child helped. Ever since I was eleven, I sold things, waited on tables, washed dishes, kneaded bread, all kinds of work. I also helped my father make out the bills. He had them written in Chinese, so all I did was record in English, since we had ten Hawaiians who used to charge at the store. And then I helped him collect.

Most of the Chinese paid their bills, but there were a few who were hard up. One family, sort of a relative of ours, had a farm in Kula, and they had several children. They said they had hard luck. One of the daughters was sick all the time. Every time they raised chickens, the chickens would die. They raised pigs, the pigs would die. So, they didn't have much money. My father gave them rice and other foods. When they left for Honolulu, they thanked my father very much, and said that maybe someday, they will pay us back. Most Chinese are trustworthy because they're ancestor worshippers, and don't want their descendants to be ashamed of them.

But certain times, Hawaiians would hide when my parents went to their house to collect. So, I would go. Because I was a little girl, you see? When I knocked, they would come to the door. When they couldn't pay, we'd stop giving them credit, and that's that. We'd just lose on it, that's all. You know, many Hawaiians in the early days often got drunk on paydays. That's why they weren't able to pay their bills. And then, after 1925, I think, we didn't have anybody charging. Everything became strictly cash.

In the early days, there weren't very many stores in Paia. So, nearly everything you would think of, we sold. Things we ourselves could use, too. We sold work clothes, especially khaki pants, khaki shirts, and *'ahina,* or denim, pants. And working shoes. And then, we sold yards of cloth so women could make dresses. For your hair, there'd be combs and brushes. There would be towels and washcloths. For your teeth, there'd be toothpaste and toothbrushes.

Because there were so many Chinese, we brought in plenty boxes of food to supply their demand. They all liked the flat salt fish which came from California. They didn't have that kind of fish in China. Chinese people could live on just rice and salt fish, just like how the Japanese live on *ume, takuan,* and sometimes, *aku,* or tuna fish. Our government didn't allow any pork sausages from China, so we bought our Chinese sausages from San Francisco and Vancouver, Canada for just about ten cents a pound. We had canned water chestnuts and bamboo shoots. Bitter melon and canned chicken. Dried duck meat from China was selling for just twenty-five cents each. So many things that it takes time to recall every item.

The train brought crates of food from Kahului Pier straight up to Paia Depot. Then my father would pick up the freight on his horse and wagon and bring it home. There weren't any macadamized roads in the early days, and I remember sometimes the wagon wheels got stuck in the mud.

We also sold rice, *poi,* fresh vegetables, and fish. In the beginning, my father got rice from Chinese farmers who came on horseback from Keanae. But they quit raising rice around 1915, saying it wasn't profitable. So they started raising taro. Till today, some of their descendants are still raising taro.

People brought their own bag or container when they came to our store to buy *poi.* We'd weigh the container, put in the *poi,* then weigh the whole thing. In those days, it was only about five cents a pound. Mostly, it was Hawaiian people who bought *poi.*

Hew's Store and Restaurant, 1930. *Courtesy Violet Hew Zane*

Some of our vegetables we got from Paia plantation families, who always found time to make use of the land around them. They lived in plantation homes, but there was quite a bit of land around. So, they planted certain things like Chinese peas, *won bok* cabbage and mustard cabbage, and brought them to the store to sell to us.

There were many Chinese in Kula in the early days, too, who raised lots of corn and other vegetables. They often came to Paia to sell vegetables, eggs and chickens to us. They'd start early in the morning on their horse and wagons, and get down here about lunch time. But they couldn't go home the same day, so they slept overnight at our place. Our house had an attic with rooms and beds, so we were running a hotel. The next morning, they bought groceries—whatever they needed —from our store because there were no grocery stores in Kula. Filled their wagons, and back home they'd go.

Our store did very well, but our restaurant did even better. We opened from 4:30 in the morning till eight o'clock at night. In those days, plantation people started to work very early. By five o'clock, as soon as they could see, they were out working. So they wanted to eat breakfast and make their lunches before they go out to work. We had to get those things ready for them. Some came in to drink coffee and have bread or pastries for breakfast.

People liked the French bread. It was delicious! We gave them free homemade butter and guava jelly. There were lots of guava trees around Paia before, you know. I helped gather guavas, and my mother would cook them, mash them up, add sugar, and make jelly out of that.

Our apple pies and coconut pies sold for only five cents each. We used fresh apples and coconuts. The coconuts were from Kauai in the beginning, and later on from the Hana district. My father put the coconuts in the oven until the shells cracked. Then he brought them out from the oven, and it was easy to take the coconut meat from the shell. Then he grated and cooked it with sugar.

But our main thing was the homemade *saimin*. My father would pound the noodles, make the sheets, and cut them by hand with the knife. Oh, he was clever with the knife. He could cut nicely and fast. People came from all over to eat our *saimin*. All different nationalities, too.

But we served mostly the Chinese people in the area. When I was growing up, there was a big Chinese community here and lots of activities. Every family had many children. Whenever they had a son, for instance, the parents would throw a big party. Back of Nagata Store there was a big community house, and about 500 people would attend. People came from all over on horse and wagon.

You ought to see the ladies. All dressed up when they went to the parties. Beautiful silk clothes, gold twenty-five-karat rings on each finger, gold earrings, bracelets, and hair ornaments. We were all dressed up, too. I remember that.

Chinese New Year's was a big celebration. We would close the restaurant and store for two days. We all dressed in our best clothes and my father took us from one Chinese house to another. We knocked at the door and wished each other Happy New Year. Then the owner of the house gave us little gifts wrapped in red paper. In the beginning, we got twenty-five cents. Then, when everything was expensive, we got only ten cents, and then nickels. The adults got tea and Chinese candies and cakes. After we were through, we went on to the next house and the next.

Then, after we got home, people came to visit us, you see? The mother never left her house. She always stayed home, cooked the food, and received the guests.

Also, in the early morning of New Year's Day, my father would burn a long string of firecrackers, filling the whole street with smoke. I remember the horses had to be taken away from the street, otherwise they would try to run away.

In the early days, the county fair, too, was an exciting event. We used to go to Kahului for the fair on a train. The plantation furnished the train, and we sat on makeshift benches. They really were cars to carry cane, you know. So we got on at Paia Depot, and got off at Kahului. Do you know where the Burger King is now located? The railroad depot was across the street.

Later on, like during World War I, there were more automobiles and trucks, so we went down on them. Our friend, a Chinese man who owned a store, had a Ford sedan. So when the war ended in 1918, we celebrated and there was a parade. Cars went from Paia to Wailuku, and we sang war songs like "Get Your Gun and Get the Kaiser," and "Keep the Home Fires Burning." All the way back, we sang, too.

And, after cars and other conveniences came in, the business got easier. In 1920, my father bought a secondhand car for about $200. He no longer had the job of feeding and bathing the horse, so he sold it.

Life was easier, too, for the farmers from Keanae and Kula when they got their trucks. They no longer had to sleep overnight in Paia. They could bring their goods in the morning, and return by lunch time.

Electricity also made life easier. We started getting electricity in 1924, so we could sell ice cream and cold soda water. My mother made and sold ice cubes, so she didn't have to wait for the ice man from Maui Soda and Ice Works. And we could keep leftovers longer; we no longer had to boil them or preserve them with salt or Chinese spices.

And my mother no longer had to clean the glass bulbs of our kerosene lamps. We called them "chimneys." Smoke and soot would come out through the chimneys, so whenever the flame was big or the wind was blowing, we couldn't get a good light. So, every morning, she had to clean about nine chimneys.

Life was getting easier with cars and electricity, but we still had to work hard. Then, about midnight, July 5, 1930, when we were fast asleep, someone yelled, "Fire, fire!" We all got up, looked out the window, and saw a fire going at the corner. Oh, we quickly picked up our things and dashed out of the house. The policeman on the road told us to get away because they were dynamiting the houses [to create firebreaks]. And the fire truck was too slow in coming from Wailuku. When it finally came, the water pressure was so low that they couldn't put out the fire.

The fire burnt all the houses on our side and across the street. Our store and restaurant was totally destroyed, except for the few things we could get out. Whatever money and jewelry we could get our hands on, we collected and rushed out. We were thinking about saving our lives.

The carpenters started work rebuilding our store and restaurant right away. We reopened three months later. My father was in a hurry to reopen because he had the family to support. You know, so many children. My father did well enough to support and educate his children. And he had enough money to visit his home in China three times. Once, when he was away for about three months, I managed the whole business. I took care of everything. When the salesmen called, I gave them the order and paid the bills. I also wrote to Honolulu for the order of Chinese goods. I did the picking up of goods at Paia Depot. All that. I worked hard when I was young. I was a husky girl.

In the old days, my father didn't want his daughters to marry other nationalities. He was very strict with me. Of course, Chinese sons could marry any nationality they wanted and, in China, have as many wives as they wanted. But the daughters were to marry only one time and no more.

I got married in 1931 to a Chinese student. We lived in Honolulu for a short while, then my husband left to attend an air college in St. Louis.

So, I came back to Maui to my parents. I was already pregnant before he left, so I gave birth the following year to twin girls. After my husband graduated from the air college, he went to China and got a job with the airlines. But my mother wouldn't let me go to China to be with him because the babies were very young. She didn't want us to risk our lives going to a place like that.

We stayed back until 1934, when my mother said, "If you want to go back now to be with your husband, you go. But don't take the girls."

So, I went to China alone, leaving my girls for my parents to look after. The following year, I gave birth to my oldest son in Hong Kong. My folks were forever asking me to come back because the girls needed my care. I was wasting my life over there, playing a lot of mahjong and things like that. Social life. Dancing and whatnot. Servants to take care of everything. I'm not used to that kind of life. I believe in working.

So I came back to Hawaii while I was pregnant with the last child in 1936. My husband never wanted to come back, so he remained there. Then came World War II, I couldn't go back to China at all. After the war, he still didn't want to come back over this way. Since I had a good profession, teaching school, and my children to support and educate, I couldn't go that way.

Time went on. He died in an air crash in the South China Sea. I never saw him again. That's the end.

But I kept myself busy during the war years. The restaurant was very, very busy. The servicemen would just run off the bus, get into the restaurant and order their food. They filled up the tables in no time.

Even though all of us were working somewhere else, we all—the family—chipped in and worked whenever we had free time. We didn't hire any outsiders because we managed to do the work. My father was old, but he could work.

Because of the blackout, my folks had to make pastries early in the morning with very little light. We kept on opening early during the war years, but we had to close early.

We never had any trouble during the war because we didn't have a bar. There were three bars in town, but two were just open for the war years. There were an additional three restaurants, but they also closed after the servicemen left because they didn't get any business.

Gradually, after the war, our restaurant and store business became less and less. It began dropping when Maui Agricultural Company, the plantation here, merged with HC&S, another plantation, in 1948. Many of the workers were scattered here and there, so we no longer got the workers during the lunch hour. And then, many moved out to live in Kahului. Stores began opening in Kahului and people did most of their shopping there.

Like us, we remained because we catered to all kinds of people. Once, when we visited our granduncle's house in Honolulu, he suggested that we sell our place, move to Honolulu and open a restaurant because we had no social life here. You see, because there were hardly any Chinese.

But then, we had three acres of land here, enough to keep us going. And our restaurant really made good all the time. That's why we never moved away. Of course, my parents said it's all right for the rest of us to go elsewhere, but they were not going to move.

I was the only one who remained with my father and mother during their last days. I took care of my mother the last three and a half years of her life. She was able to walk around and feed herself. But I had to see to it that she got her food every meal, and that she got her bath, and the laundry done. My father, too, could walk around. I saw to it that he's comfortable and clean. They were very fortunate that they were not bed invalids like some elderly people that have to be cared for like children.

My father didn't pass the business on to me, because I didn't ask for it. I was already teaching. My brother Patrick, who was just discharged from the army in 1949, wanted to take over the business because my father made good. And he also made good.

My daughters graduated high school in 1950 and left for the Mainland. My brothers and sisters got married and moved out. So, that left only me and two boys until they graduated high school. The first one joined the army, and the second one went to the Mainland for school. For two years, there was nobody in this house except me. You know, I just worked hard over at the restaurant. I helped nights after teaching during the day, and on weekends, holidays, and vacations. I didn't feel anything, because I'm used to working. I guess I enjoy it.

After Patrick died in 1975, he passed it to his wife, who came from Honolulu. She just opens the business for a short time during the day only. After she goes, I guess she'll pass it on to her family, since she has no children. I don't think she'll pass it back to the Hews. So, the Hews lost out.

I think I'll live the rest of my life in Paia. I have my state pension and social security to look after me. We have a Chinese cemetery where I can be buried free, because in the early days, a Chinese club put up the money and bought ten acres of land for the purpose of burying Chinese people and their dependents and descendants. So, myself and most of the family will be buried in this Chinese cemetery.

Osame Manago
FARMER'S DAUGHTER, IMMIGRANT BRIDE

ESOHP

Osame Nagata Manago was born on April 16, 1891, in a farming community in Fukuoka-*ken*, Japan. Having no brothers, Osame and her four sisters planted and harvested rice, and did many of the chores traditionally assigned to sons. Told she was educated enough for a farmer's daughter, Osame left school after the fifth grade.

She was one of some 14,000 picture brides immigrating to Hawaii in the 1907–1923 period. Picture bride marriages were arranged in Japan by the parents or go-betweens of single Japanese men working in Hawaii. The prospective couple exchanged photographs and letters. If both sides agreed to the marriage, it was legalized by adding the woman's name to the man's family register.

Osame met her husband Kinzo Manago at the immigration station upon her arrival in Hawaii in 1913. In earlier years, marriage ceremonies were required to take place in the station, but this rule was dropped. Osame and Kinzo were married at the Izumo Taisha, a Shinto shrine. The picture bride period ended when the Immigration Act of 1924 was enacted by Congress, barring the immigration of all aliens not eligible for citizenship.

Kinzo brought Osame to Kona where he worked as a cook for the Wallace family. To supplement her husband's income, Osame did a variety of jobs, including sorting coffee beans for the Captain Cook Coffee Mill and embroidering linens.

Shortly after the first of their eight children was born in 1915, Osame and Kinzo opened a coffee shop, specializing in homemade bread and *udon,* or noodles. The coffee shop evolved into the Manago Hotel. The patronage of order-takers from wholesale companies during the 1930s and of soldiers during World War II enabled the Managos to keep the hotel open. The Managos operated the hotel for more than fifty years until Kinzo's death in 1967. The hotel is now managed by Osame's son Harold, but Osame, by choice, continues to work in the kitchen, laundry and garden of Manago Hotel.

Osame Manago was selected to be recorded for the 1980 "A Social History of Kona" project. She was interviewed in Japanese by Michi Kodama-Nishimoto, a bilingual researcher-interviewer. The first interview session with Osame was held in her daughter's Honolulu condominium; the second at the Manago Hotel in Captain Cook, Kona. Michi recalls sitting with Osame on the floor of Osame's bedroom in Kona, poring over old photographs. Osame spoke a Southern Japanese dialect and would gesture frequently with work-roughened hands. As she talked, Osame seemed to be reliving her experiences—her face and voice recording the remembered feelings.

The emotional impact of Osame's recollections was retained in the interview translations, from which the narrative was edited. It is an unusually personal account, with historical events such as the immigration experience, depression, and World War II seen through Osame's eyes.

MY PARENTS really had a hard time raising us five girls, all girls. They used to have a son, but he died on the 15th of August of the year he turned eighteen. His name was Sataro . . . he died at night of a high fever, I heard. We used to have a big field, about half an acre. Anyway, my parents went out there, stepping in his footprints, which were clear when all the water dried up. They were trying to feel Sataro's feet. This is what I heard. I also heard that he was a good singer and when people heard him sing, they used to say, "That's Sataro-*san* singing, he must be going to the field." But, I didn't know my brother, since I was born much later. He was the second child; I was the fourth, born on the 16th of April, in Meiji 24 (1891). But, I remember my father always saying, "I wish he were still alive. If only he were still alive."

My father used to say that he felt sorry for us girls since he didn't have a son. But we worked as much as men. We didn't fall behind in our work just because we were women. We didn't need *kōkua* from others. We *kōkua* each other. We used to plan when to work, and where to work, by ourselves.

We grew rice, only rice. The rice field was about three acres. And there was a small field to grow vegetables. People used to tell me enviously that we were lucky to have that field to grow potatoes and squash. My mother grew those vegetables and often used to distribute them to neighbors.

But, the rice . . . we made good rice. In our time, in Fukuoka-*ken*, we would plant rice seedlings one by one along ropes which were set from one end of the field to the other. When we had five people working together, we had five rows being planted at the same time. And the field had to look neat horizontally, vertically, and diagonally. Finishing one line, we went on to the next, after measuring it correctly. When we came to the end of the field, the work was completed.

After four weeks or so, the seedlings which had looked so fragile would settle more securely in the soil. Then we had to weed. If people did not work hard, the grass grew tall. Since there weren't any chemicals to kill weeds like nowadays, we had to weed by hand and soon lost our fingernails.

And, in those days, we had a horse. We used to spread its dung on thick straw mats, and dry it for manure in the field. We also used human feces. Not now, but in those days, we used it as fertilizer. We would buy and carry it in a cart. We called it *shirimochi: shiri* for "buttocks" and *mochi* for "rice cakes." We took people some rice in return for the manure.

Then, after three to four weeks, the ground got hard, preventing the plants' roots from growing. So we used a coal rake and turned the soil over. And, after about three weeks, we started from the opposite side, making the entire field soft. We used to do this twice and our faces became wet and sticky with mud. But we had to do this, since we were farmers. And there were leeches, the kind which stick to you and suck your blood. That was the way it was, when I was young.

And, about September or so, the plants would have finished growing and they would have grain. All the water which had been vital for the rice to grow would be gone to the river, and the ground would be dry and hard. The rice would turn yellow and plump by the end of October. It was beautiful to see them, waving and rustling in the wind *sara-sara, sara-sara*. We used to say, "Oh, what a beautiful crop," while looking at our rice, which was better than our neighbors'. But when a typhoon hit the rice paddies, the plants would fall. When a typhoon didn't hit, they would grow beautifully.

The rice harvest began when the ground became dry and hard. We used sickles, like this, using both hands, putting the plants we cut aside. Two or three days later, we tied them together with ropes or straw. Then I carried the rice stalks on my shoulder to this place where there was something like a table with holes; and women were working around it, pounding the grain off the stalks. After they had pounded it, my father used to toss the stalks over to the side.

About the time we had pounded about ten sacks of rice off the stalks, the sun was usually setting. It used to get windy at this time, and, taking advantage of this wind, my father and us, my sisters, worked together: my father threshed the rice, shaking the rice stalks, and the wind blew the hulls away; and we sisters measured the rice and put it into sacks, tying each with a rope. We put those sacks, sometimes five or even eight sacks, on the cart and went home.

After supper, we would go out to work again and in the field we'd line up the cut rice stalk bundles and tie them securely with straw so that the rain or wind would not affect them. That was our night work, under the moon. It was after that work that we came home, finally took a bath, and went to bed. My father didn't like for us to work too late into the night and be late for work in the morning. So we would tell him to go on ahead, take a bath and go to bed early.

He used to say, "Are you going out to work again?"

We would say, "Yes, a little while, since it's as bright as daytime with the moon up like this. We can't waste it staying at home doing nothing."

We felt sorry for my father since all he had were daughters. So we worked hard. We almost worked twenty-four hours a day. We'd work until late at night wearing *koshimaki,* kimono underskirts. When most girls were out wearing nice clothes, my father wanted me to work hard instead.

Whether I was working in the rice paddy or vegetable field, I worked so hard that I didn't care how I looked. People used to call me "Nagata's Onagoyama," as if I were a *sumō* wrestler. I would go into the mountains to collect firewood, which was hard to find. Even at night, I would cart it to our house and toss the wood to my sister who was standing on the second floor. She caught and stored it. Although I was not very big and had a difficult time unloading the firewood, I would manage to get enough to fill the storage area.

Thinking of the hard work I did as a youngster, I didn't think I would be able to marry into a good family. I disliked farming and thought of it as a harsh life. But my mother was kind to me. She would sell rice to a middleman to get money to secretly make me a kimono or two; so I felt obligated to stay as a farmer. Because of her, I couldn't leave home. All my friends were farmers' daughters, but they left home and worked at shops or restaurants. I was the only one who stayed home and did farming, since my father told me that a farmer's daughter should remain a farmer.

"You are only a farmer's daughter. What good does it do to get more education for working in the fields or for business? If you can sign your name, that's enough." That is what my father said. My neighbor was a doctor, and his daughter, a friend of mine, was going to high school. So I wanted to go, too. My father said people would laugh at me if I, a farmer's daughter, went to high school. But he allowed me to go to the fifth grade. So I did.

After that, as I was a girl, I was taught how to sew and do other tasks, since that was what we were expected to do. I don't mean to brag about it, but I at least learned how to sew clothes for myself. My hometown is famous for *kasuri*, a kimono material, and I learned how to weave this properly from my sister. Also, my mother taught me how to make *shibori*, a material which is tie-dyed. I learned these things in winter, when we farmers did not work in the fields. There were many different kinds of kimonos in Japan, not to mention the different kinds of *obi*, or sashes. My mother taught me all these things, since she wanted me to learn them before I got married.

My parents wanted us to marry into good homes. They had to marry us off according to our ages, the older ones first. Since my oldest sister died, the second one took a *yōshi*, a husband who takes his wife's family name, to carry on our family name. The next one married, and so did the one next to her. And since we were all well known as hard workers, even when we were still very young, rich farmers came to ask us to marry into their families, though we were not the greatest beauties.

I got married for the first time when I was seventeen. My father had a brother, and they were the only sons in his family. I was married to my father's brother's, that is my uncle's, wife's nephew. I didn't want to marry him. He was a handsome man, but I didn't quite like him. I just didn't feel comfortable with him. I actually disliked him. My parents told me I could come back if I couldn't stand him, but I should stay for at least three days. I was crying and crying, I didn't want to marry him, but I had to, to save my father's face and the relationship between my father and his brother. It was something like I was stolen from my family temporarily, so it was not a legal marriage, but a trial one. Since it was a trial marriage, we simply exchanged *sakazuki, sake* in ceremonial nuptial cups. And I didn't wear formal clothes, just everyday ones . . . that was it.

I came back home three days later, lying to the groom's family that I was going to the toilet. I opened the door to go out, although there was a toilet in the house. I really didn't want to stay. I hated that place so much that I thought all my anger and hatred would gush out. That was a night with a full moon. It was September, and the soldiers were practicing war in the field and making a lot of noise, *pata-pata-pata, pata-pata-pata,* that scared me a lot. And there was a cemetery on the way back to my home. Although I was scared of the soldiers and the cemetery, I told myself I had to go home.

I got home about midnight and tried to open the door to the main room, calling, "Mom, Mom." Probably my mom had been worrying about me.

She called my name, "Is that you, Osame?"

I said, "Yes, it's me."

She was glad to see me home, and as she opened the door she said, "Oh, you are home, it's all right, it's all right. It must have been hard for you. I'm sorry that you had to go through this, but it's all right, now you're home."

I felt bad for my parents after I came home, because the groom's family home was so close, and they all belonged to the same temple we did. Since our field and theirs were next to each other, we had to work far away from them, so they wouldn't see us.

I thought I should have stayed with the groom but I just couldn't help disliking the guy. That's why I told my mother that I wanted to leave Japan and go somewhere far away from home. My mother tried to comfort me, saying I shouldn't say things like that, and there would be other chances to marry somebody nicer. But I insisted that I should go somewhere far away, somewhere like Hawaii. My elder sister's husband, who was a *yōshi,* had left for Hawaii island when their baby was thirty days old, and had been missing since then. So I wanted to come here and find him for my sister. Besides, my parents were having a hard time with the relatives because of me. I thought if I'd gone somewhere far away, my father and uncle would forget about me and get along again. I was ashamed for my father and wanted to work very hard in Hawaii. And if and when I should go back to Japan, I wanted people to look up to me. That's why I came to Hawaii.

I don't know how the Managos knew about me, but they wanted me as a bride for their second son, Kinzo. They thought I was a hard worker and suited for the Manago family, I guess, although I was not the greatest beauty. My husband's family was pretty rich, so when I said that I would marry him, my father's brother was not very happy, saying that our family didn't match up with Manago's. But he said to my father to go ahead if that was what my father wanted to do. So my father's brother didn't attend the wedding ceremony, which was a splendid ceremony, but a proxy one. It was a wedding by photograph—a *shashin kekkon*. I only looked at my husband's picture. I couldn't meet him in person because he was in Hawaii at that time. After the proxy ceremony I stayed with the Managos for ten months in the city of Kurume, where there was a big military camp. The Managos' estate was so big, to go to the military camp we didn't have to step on anybody else's property; it was all theirs. I stayed until I came to Honolulu on the *Siberia*, a small ship, 18,000 tons. My parents came to Nagasaki to see me off.

I was thinking about nothing but coming to Hawaii; I didn't think about anything else. At the physical inspection in Nagasaki, my eyes were fine, but I had hookworms. So I was suspended in Nagasaki for a week. My mother went home, leaving my father with me, saying she would be back when I got rid of the hookworms. She came back a few days later. At the inspection site, where we had our stool examined, a person gave me somebody else's stool, which didn't have hookworms. The person told me to keep it in my *obi* and switch it with my own stool. But a *haole*, a white person, was watching me when I was using the bathroom, so it was impossible to switch, you know? I couldn't even urinate. So I gave up and took my own to be inspected. A person who'd come back from America, who helped arrange my going to Hawaii, told me to eat a lot of nuts which apparently made it difficult for the microscope to find the worms. So I ate quite a lot of these nuts which my mother roasted for me. And I must have been lucky; I was told there weren't any hookworms, so I passed. My mother and father filled up a *shingenbukuro*, cloth pouch, with persimmons, pears, candies, and rice crackers, and so many other goodies. They said I would be on board for one week to ten days, would be lonely, and should eat all of the fruits and treats.

When I got on board, the odor was so bad I couldn't possibly eat anything. I got seasick and felt so bad I couldn't eat. They told me to lie down where there were hammocks all lined up. There were also beds—small, thin *futon*, or comforters, on cots made of iron. There was a woman sleeping next to me, and since she didn't get seasick, I asked her to eat what I had. While lying down, feeling sick, I had to listen to her eating, an awful crunching sound, *gari-gari, gari-gari.* But there was nothing I could do except to comfort myself. I thought she deserved the food since she'd been taking care of me, bringing water for me, and I might as well give the food away; otherwise, they'd be thrown away anyway. A person named Nagata from Kumamoto-*ken* was very kind and brought me some *udon* noodles. She said it was a good thing to eat when seasick. She also brought some medicine for seasickness when I couldn't even raise my head. She told me what day it was and how many more days it was going to take to get to Hawaii. Since I didn't sleep well days and nights, I felt that I had been bedridden for a month.

On the ninth or tenth day, I guess, she came and told me that we were to land the next day. She took me to the deck and told me not to look behind, but forward; she told me that the cool wind would make me feel better. She brought me *Pake manju,* Chinese buns with bean-jam filling, and water. She was so kind to me that I felt happy. She told me that we'd be arriving tomorrow and that there was a bath on the boat, so I should clean myself up a little. She was so nice to me. And there was Misao-*san,* who now lives in Hamakua but was from a town close to my own hometown. She also came to see me, to help choose what kimono I should wear when I got off the boat, and she took the kimono out of the *yanagi-gōri,* or willow suitcase, for me. So I landed.

I landed at Honolulu. But I had to stay at the immigration station in this dark and spacious house. There I was told by Mr. Tomizo Katsunuma that the boat to Hawaii island had just left, and it would have to make a circle before coming back to Honolulu to pick me up, and that would be two weeks later. He told me to be patient. So there I was, having to wait for the boat. There was another person who'd come earlier and was waiting for the Hawaii island boat, too. So the two of us were left in this huge place. We slept in beds that were like shelves for silkworms. Every day, for two weeks, having nothing to do, we looked out the window, wishing for the boat to come. We saw trains with smoke coming out of their smokestacks, making some kind of big noise. This *kanaka jii-san,* a Hawaiian old man, a janitor, came to clean up the place. I couldn't understand what he was saying, you know? We just felt so bad that we regretted we'd come, and felt we wouldn't have if we had known what it would be like. We were saying that. But the two weeks passed, and since the boat was coming the next day, Mr. Katsunuma came to tell us, "Fukuoka-*ken* people, tomorrow, they're coming so you shouldn't worry."

Finally the day came. Somebody told me there was a man with a broad forehead and another one a bit shorter, and he asked me which one would be my husband. I had my husband's picture with me, so I showed it to him. He said, "Oh, this one, with the broad forehead, who looks intelligent. This one has the air of a businessman." And, then my husband and I were introduced to each other by Mr. Katsunuma. He told us that I had come all the way to Hawaii, so we should take care of each other and work hard. He made us hold each other's hand there. After we left the place, we went to a shrine, Izumo Taisha, where we, two couples, had a ceremony conducted by a Shinto priest. We exchanged marriage *sakazuki*. Then we went to Fukuoka-*ya,* a hotel, and stayed there for two days, waiting for the boat to the Big Island.

During those first days with my husband, I said to him that I came all the way from Japan to be with him, and that his parents had told me to bring him back. I said I was going to work hard so I could take him back to Japan as soon as possible. He said that he was going to work hard in order to get back and that he'd been feeling sorry for deceiving his parents in coming here. He said we should work hard together. He also said he wouldn't have come if he'd known he was to stay in Hawaii, that he originally left Japan to go to Canada, and that he'd worried his parents. He said his dreams hadn't come true. He was saying that. It seemed that he really had wanted to go to Canada to study English.

My husband had a cousin in Canada. When my husband finished high school, he applied to go to Canada to study English but kept this secret from the family. When his parents found out, they tried to stop him, saying he should stay home, that he had no reason to go to Canada. But he wanted to go, once he was accepted. So he left home with four or five of his friends.

When they landed in Honolulu, where they had to change ships and were waiting temporarily, one of his friends gambled away money that he had borrowed from my husband. They were all stuck without even a nickel. They stayed at Fukuoka-*ya* that night and Manago wrote a letter to his cousin in Canada. The cousin sent twenty dollars in gold right away and he used it as pocket money in Honolulu. And this friend who had lost the money in gambling disappeared without repaying. My husband was at a loss and asked at Fukuoka-*ya* if there was anybody from Fukuoka that he knew. Through Fukuoka-*ya,* my husband discovered that he did have a relative, named Shikada-*san,* on Hawaii. So my husband got the address and decided to go there.

I think he landed at Ka'u, not Hilo. He landed at a place in Ka'u with a name that sounded like "Honuapo." It was very stormy, so stormy that he had to be taken by the hand to get off the boat, so he told me. And he went to see Shikada-*san* in Kona. Then he stayed with

Mrs. Shikada's brother, Nishimura-*san,* off and on and became friends by the time I arrived. He also became a cook for Mr. Wallace, a white person, and after he saved some money, he called me over from Japan.

We left Honolulu for Kona that day at noon. But our boat was something else. We were put together with horses and cattle. I only kept wondering how could we go on a boat like that. I remember it clearly —the cow dung and all. I asked my husband if that was how we were going. And it was. I went sitting on the boards, leaning against my *yanagi-gōri.* We couldn't lie down, we had to be sitting up all the way to Kona. My husband told me that everything, people, cattle, cargo went together, and even if you asked, there was no more room. The boat arrived offshore of Kona, and a canoe, you know, a little boat, came to get us. They handed me down to the canoe with a count of "One, two, three." They did the same to my husband and to my *yanagi-gōri.*

In Kailua, there was a landing, made of lumber; that's where the canoe landed. The canoe was lower than the landing, so they pulled my hands while the others pushed me up, and I came out of the canoe. That's how we came in those days. It was really pitiful. Really. And for the cattle and horses, they tied them by the neck to the canoe and let them swim, then they would lift them up.

So we arrived at Kailua about six o'clock in the morning. There was a small restaurant. We rested there for a while. We waited for a person who was supposed to come and pick us up. Since I had been told that there would be a celebration party, I washed my face, changed into my lilac *montsuki,* crested kimono, with a pretty *obi,* and was ready to go. Then a man came down with a horse and carriage with four poles standing up. I was told to hold onto a pole since the road was rough and full of rocks. Guava tree branches hit the carriage, *Batan! Batan! Batan!* We were told not to stick our faces out since we'd get hurt. Really it was terrible. When we got up to Captain Cook, it was twelve o'clock noon.

So we arrived at a place a little beyond ours, near where Nishimura-*san* was staying. Because it was a wedding celebration, everybody was waiting for us. They stood in front of the house, saying "Welcome back, Mr. Manago," to my husband, and "Welcome, you must be exhausted!" to me. When the party started, it was just like Japan. Everybody was dancing and singing, just having a jolly good time. Everybody was very kind to me from the time I arrived.

The next morning we went on foot to introduce me to the Wallaces, where my husband was working. There wasn't a car then so we walked. The Wallaces were a couple and their daughter. I was welcomed there, too. They were so pleased to see me that they hugged and patted me many times, saying "Good bride, good bride." (Chuckles) They told me to think of their house as Manago's house, and told me to come back again soon.

My husband worked at the Wallaces for five or six years. They really trusted him. And after I got married to him, I got pregnant with my first baby. It was in 1915. During the delivery, Mrs. Wallace was with me, massaging my back, telling me that this part of the waist was supposed to hurt when the baby was coming out. The missus—the *haole* lady—kept massaging and telling me, "It'll be finished soon since your back is hurting so much," or something like that. I didn't understand what she was saying since it was in English, you know. My husband was told to stay with me since the delivery was taking a long time.

And after this coffee farm woman came, she helped me. She told me not to worry and told me what to do. She held me from behind firmly, right here around the waist. After she made me sit up, the baby came out with a rush. But really, my back hurt so much that I wished it could be cut off. I heard that boy babies would make your back hurt more than girl babies would, but I never knew it would hurt that much. The baby was born about thirty minutes after the coffee farm woman came, on the 20th of August, the day of Odaishi-*san*, a festival day. When I was delivering him, I was cursing boys, since my back was hurting so much—but after he was born, I was so thankful. Luckily the baby was a healthy one and my delivery was easy. And, it was my first delivery . . .

I rested for a couple of weeks and started working little by little. Mr. Wallace was a *luna,* or foreman, at a big plantation, and he had a couple of horses. Mrs. Wallace and her daughter used to go out on horseback since they didn't have a car then. And those horses were tied in a large field. To help with the work at the Wallaces', I used to pick up horse dung and throw it away. But the baby was growing, and he started to crawl. I used to tie him to two places outside with my *obi,* and go to pick up horse *kūkae,* dung. And people could hear my baby cry. My husband would come to tell me that the baby was crying. But I wanted to finish cleaning the area. When I went back to the baby, he had cried himself to sleep, and his diaper was soaked. I felt so sorry for him.

Mrs. Wallace felt sorry, too, and gave me a new job, embroidering. She brought yarn to me and taught me how to do it. When I had finished a few napkins and handkerchiefs, my husband took them to her. He told her he wasn't sure if the work was satisfactory, but if it was, I would be glad to do some more. Pretty soon I was doing big tablecloths for those English people. Mrs. Wallace brought me many different kinds of work and sometimes she gave me ten dollars, other times, five dollars. I told her I was doing it because I wanted to practice embroidering and didn't want any money. I was just glad that I could be some help to her, you know. But it seems she insisted on the pay, so my husband brought home the money.

But when my baby started to crawl, and then to walk, I couldn't keep those things white, they got dirty since he would sometimes touch them; besides, the material was so thin, anyway. So I asked my husband if there were any other jobs, since now the baby had grown to crawl.

Then a woman came and asked if I'd like to sort coffee beans at Napoopoo for the Captain Cook Coffee Company. But I wasn't sure if I could do it. She told me it would be different from sewing kimonos, but better for the baby. So I went with two other women—*oba-san-ta-chi*. It was quite a long walk. I used to leave about seven o'clock in the morning, carrying my year-old baby on my back. I would fix *dango*, dumplings, for him and a *bentō* for myself. Mrs. Fukuda, Mrs. Nakamoto and myself, all three of us *oba-san-tachi* went down below Marumoto's from the upper road to the lower steep gravel road. On the way we passed coffee trees and guava, and sometimes slid down, *goro-goro-goro,* two to three feet. When we got down, we walked about a quarter of a mile to Napoopoo School. Then we had to walk down to the mill. It took two hours to go down the first part, then to Napoopoo School, and finally another hour to go down to the mill.

Mostly Japanese women worked; there was one Hawaiian. Those Japanese women had their own houses in the coffee company camp. They worked all year long, along with their husbands. But I only went there because I heard about the job and worked there about a month.

Sometimes, at the mill our kids fought with others. Since we didn't live there and the other coffee sorters did, we felt awkward when they fought. So we used to tie our kids to the table with our *obi*. And our three kids, who were from up the hill, would play together. The Napoopoo resident workers told us things like, "Those kids who came from up the hill have a strong odor even in their urine." So we used to tell our kids to stay with us. We ate our *bentō* there. And we had to go up the hill when we went home, carrying our kids on our backs. That was difficult, since we worked so hard sorting coffee beans.

We used to get thirty-five cents for sorting a bag full of coffee beans, some of which were squashed or split in half, or crumbled, and so on. It was thirty-five cents for one bag sorted. I could hardly do two bags. When the boss found one bad coffee bean in a finished bag, I had to do it all over again, emptying the bag. So I ended up working over one bag twice, when I could have worked on two. It was really miserable at times like that. But, the three of us used to comfort each other in our hard work, "*Yare, yare, kyō yatta, no?* (Well, well, we really did it today, didn't we)?" And, it was only seventy cents a day, not to mention the troubles I had—the kids and the long walk. Finally, people told us that we three women should quit. So we all did.

Shortly after that, my husband told me we should go to Honolulu. That was all right with me. When my husband told his boss, Mr. Wallace, that he wanted to go to Honolulu, the boss said that we didn't have to go to Honolulu, that we had a child to consider, and that we should start a coffee shop here instead of leaving. Mr. Wallace brought us a hundred dollars, and with that money, my husband bought some flour, sugar, and other supplies, and learned how to make *udon,* and such. In Honaunau, my husband bought a house in which coffee beans used to be dried. He paid ninety dollars for it. We remodeled the house, dividing it into two parts, one for our bedroom, the other with a sink and table for making and selling *udon.* we bought a tiny stove, I can't remember exactly how much my husband paid for it, but I think it was some thirty or forty dollars. That's how we started.

We baked bread, about ten loaves a day sometimes, and we served *udon* and coffee. We used to calculate our profits, which were two to three dollars at the end of each day. After he found Maezato-*san* as his replacement at the Wallaces' my husband came here to assist with the shop. Since we didn't have gas or electricity then, we used lamps. And, we needed firewood for the stove. So both of us had to work hard. Meanwhile, our bread sold well. We used to sell out all ten loaves in one day. We served two slices of bread with jam, since we didn't have butter, with a cup of coffee. Even *udon,* of the ten or twenty servings we made, all would be sold. So we started with bread, *udon,* and coffee, and made money at first.

Above our houselot, there was a stable where there were a lot of bachelors, but not so many women. I used to do some laundry for them when I went to take my bath. I paid for the bath and did the laundry with the leftover water. I washed a shirt for five cents, three underpants for ten cents. Being bachelors, they would wear the same underwear for ten days, you know. I washed those things. A lot of our coffee shop customers were the bachelors who worked at the stable. They used to come when they were hungry and have some *udon* or coffee. After we started our shop, they first came on Sundays, just to see what it was like. There weren't any shops like ours there then, so it was convenient for them when they didn't want to cook at home. My husband sometimes had to

Manago Hotel, c. 1920s. *Courtesy Osame Manago*

make extra *udon* when we sold out the twenty *udon* we'd made for the day. He used to say, "Really, did we sell that many today? Okay, I'll start making some more," and he'd start making it.

When the shop work was done for the evening, my husband and I washed the laundry and I did the ironing. There were mechanics who worked at the big garage at Captain Cook. We washed their clothes, too, since their own missus didn't want to wash them, they were so greasy. We used hot water with soap, which wasn't white like nowadays, but red and so big that we had to cut them in pieces. We worked so hard that sometimes we didn't know the difference between day and night. Since the wholesale coffee price paid to Kona's farmers was good, people had money and they came to have coffee, *udon* and bread. Little by little, we made more profit from five dollars to ten dollars a day, like that.

When our second girl was born, I couldn't manage taking care of her and the kitchen at the same time, not to mention finding room to sleep. So we had to build another room, which we made our bedroom. That was much better than before, having more space. There were two bedrooms, a kitchen, and a place where we served coffee and *udon*. One bench was all there was, so on one end somebody drank coffee, and on the other end, somebody else ate *udon*. Above our houselot there used to be a large Paris Hotel. People would come to Kona to sell all sorts of things but their drivers couldn't stay with them at that hotel. Since they didn't have any place to stay, they asked me if they could stay at our shop for a cheap price. So we bought small single beds and put them in the extra space we had, and started letting those drivers stay. That's how we first started the Manago Hotel, back in 1917.

When the rooms were full, we put *futon*, or Japanese-style bedding, on the floor for others to sleep on. I told my husband that this is a good business, and that we should add a second floor to have more rooms. And we divided one room into two, with six *tatami*, or straw mats, in the front room. We advertised that we had a Japanese room. It became popular and everybody came. When people had to have meetings, such as the American Factors, Theo H. Davies and Co., or coffee farmers, they met and ate at our place. There was a painter who was from Nii-gata-*ken*, who was a very good cook. I asked him if he wanted to help our restaurant when he was free. He said he would. We offered him free room and board. With his help, ten to twenty people started having parties at our place. Business was very good, and we started selling *sake*, beer and other things. After work, coffee picking, people started coming to have a drink, since it was cold in the evenings, you know. Our business was growing, little by little.

To stay at our hotel in those days it was one dollar a day. Mostly Japanese stayed at our hotel. And also Portuguese, *gaijin*, who came with big trucks of samples for the big shops; they were very strong. They were from Theo H. Davies wholesalers.

Some people came with lots of twenty-dollar bills when they had a bonus at the sugar plantation. About seven of them used to come in one truck, taking a whole day to get to our place from Honokaa. They would have supper at our place, buy some *bentō*, and go on to Hilo. It took a day to get to Hilo. They went from Hilo to Honokaa, where they stayed overnight, and spent one more night elsewhere as they went around the island. It took four nights to make a round trip of the island. The roads were rough, with lots of rocks. In those days, the tires were airless, not like the ones nowadays. That's the way it was.

Thanks to customers who spread the word that they could eat good food any time at the Managos', we were doing pretty well. And when the Kona coffee business got big, several companies from Hilo, Honolulu and elsewhere started sending more of their order-takers to Kona.

Finally, in 1929, we went to Japan. We were able to go since we had some money saved up through all our hard work. My father sent me a letter saying he wanted to see our children. So I told my husband about it and he said it would be a good idea, that we would get some help for the hotel, although it was busy. Mr. Yonekura, who was with the *Hawaii Hochi,* offered to watch over the management. We hired cooks. We asked a friend of ours, Ishida-*san,* who was a teacher at Napoopoo School, to become the manager. We told them that they didn't have to make money, all they had to do was to keep the business going. Mr. Frank Arakawa, a construction engineer who happened to be staying at our hotel, offered to help take care of the place while we were gone. He also sent us some documents which we needed to come back from Japan. Since we would be gone during April, May and June, we had to take both winter and summer clothes. We took three trunks and a suitcase, some of which were filled with clothes I ordered from Honolulu and Hilo through order-takers. My eldest was fourteen, and the youngest of the six children, a seven-month-old, I carried.

Kyushu is detached from Honshu, and in those days there was a steamboat transport between the two islands. In order to get to Kyushu, we had to get on this steamboat. And after we crossed the sea, we took a train. There were lots of people waiting to greet us at the station. They praised us for our determined effort to bring the children back home. They told us they were glad to see us all, and to see that all six children and the two of us had made it all right. As for my father, he was so excited about receiving my husband in his home for the first time that he had readied my husband's Japanese-style formal wear and a set of kimono for me. My father said that seeing the children was worth more than a house fiiled with gold, and he cried, even though he was a man.

Although we planned to stay three months, a month or so after our happy arrival, I received letters from Hawaii telling us that there was a hotel being built next to ours. Our friends wrote, warning that the new hotel builders were going to take our business away, that we had to get back home as soon as we could. I told my husband that we must get back home, since we didn't want our friends to worry. And I thought my father was satisfied now that he had seen all our children, although we'd been there only a month.

But they'd had a small family, just my parents and my sister and her husband, with no child. When the eight of us came, the house was cheerful and full of people. My mother said to me that she wouldn't know what to do when we were gone, that it would be like a typhoon had gone by. She begged me to stay, asking if I really had to go. I told her that I had to go because of the letter, and that I would come back again after the kids got bigger.

Before we left my parents, we had a farewell dinner at my sister's house. After we got back from my sister's, we noticed something was going on in the main room of my father's house. We heard singing and wondered what was happening. It was my parents singing for my little one. They had a pair of *zori*, or sandals, made for my little one by an eighty-eight-year-old man, who by custom symbolized longevity. It was a ceremony to wish her a long life. My father and mother were glad that the ceremony was conducted, and they said that the child would live long.

When we left, we had to hire two to three cars in order to get everybody in, with all the luggage. My little one was asleep in my arms when my sister came and said that the baby was so young that she couldn't tell who her mother was, that I should leave her with my mother. My sister said my mother would feel so sad when we left that Mother would go crazy or become sick. And she took my baby and carried her away into a nearby shrine. I felt then that I shouldn't have come back if I'd known that I would have to leave my baby behind. I didn't know what to do.

But, I realized how sad my mother was, and understood how she felt about my children. After all, I had many children; I thought I could leave one child with her. I told myself it would be okay. Since we had to hurry, we left for Kurume Station. My sisters came along with us to Kyoto. They came because they thought I would be lonely, leaving my baby behind. In Kyoto, when my milk dripped through my thin kimono, my sisters cried, saying that the baby must be hungry. They were so sorry for the baby and me. So without telling me, my sister called home to check on the baby. My mother apparently told my sister that the baby had drunk milk and was sleeping soundly. When my sister told me the baby was doing okay, I thought, as long as she was drinking milk, she should be all right.

After staying in Kyoto for a week, we went to Yokohama, where we were to get on a ship. When we were about to leave for Hawaii, my sisters asked me whether my sister's husband should bring the baby to Yokohama. I told them I was sure that the baby was going to be cared for very well since the baby was the only child in the house. I told them I must give her away. I was very sad, but I also thought of the time I left my mother many years ago to come to Hawaii. I owed her for that, and I had to pay her back.

Once in a while, though, I thought of the child, and imagined how she was doing; and I felt I shouldn't have gone to Japan. They often sent me pictures of the child, telling me how well she was growing, thanks to my parents and sisters.

When we got back to Hawaii, the competitor's hotel had been built, and they were having noisy parties. Mr. Frank Arakawa told me he would draw a design for the hotel and help us to expand. He brought the design and said we should buy the neighboring coffee land from the owner, Mori-*san*. Mori-*san* said, "All right, I'll cut down the coffee trees and you may have as much land as you want." So we took the land between this house and that house. We shared the street between our hotel and the competitor's, each giving five feet. This is the house we built then, without leaving any of the land empty.

We had a coffee field below our hotel, so we were going to get a mortgage on the land from a bank in order to build our hotel. But a person, whom my husband leased the land to, had taken the land document to American Factors and had borrowed money on it. We were very upset, but there was nothing we could do. So we started a *tanomoshi*. We decided to make thirty shares at ten dollars a piece.

But people told us they would be our guarantors, and encouraged us to borrow money from a bank instead. So we borrowed money from Bank of Hawaii and started building. Theo H. Davies, American Factors and other contractors made bids. After seeing the design that Mr. Arakawa had drawn, which showed rooms here and there, Davies got the contract. They understood we didn't have much money, since we had just made a trip to Japan; and they offered a deal where we wouldn't have to pay for the lumber right then, but would pay later, with a little interest. And the bank agreed to the deal.

For the actual building, Yamane-*san* was the contractor for Davies, and we paid some $20,000 to add a new hotel to the old one. We provided room and board to the carpenter and other workers and paid daily wages. We also told them they must build without our having to stop our hotel business.

But then the wholesale price of coffee, which was once seventeen cents to nineteen cents per pound, went way down, to ten cents. Nobody was buying, and many people wanted to quit the coffee farming business. We were living on their coffee business, you know. We were in trouble, and finally my husband went to work for a *haole* who lived beside the road to Napoopoo. My husband left early in the morning and didn't come home until eight o'clock at night. His salary was twenty-eight dollars a month.

At this *haole* home there was an unmarried *haole*, Wallace's *aikāne*,

Osame Manago (in window) and family, c. 1920s. *Courtesy Osame Manago*

or friend. David Paris, it was. My husband started doing laundry for him. So he used to wash and sometimes iron at night, while I was cooking for our children.

The children, four or five of them when they got old enough, started to work picking coffee at Goto-*san*'s place after school. They either helped at home or went to pick coffee, since money was money, even if they could pick only one bag full. We used to send them to work again after they had had supper, to dry the coffee after it was washed. And at home we told them to dry the dishes, and sweep and mop. They bathed the young ones and helped them get ready for school the next day. They had their clothes ready, next to their pillows, before they went to bed. We let the boys do girls' work also. We let them do everything, even wash and iron. And we were all so busy that my daughters sometimes didn't bathe for four or five days. Some people told us that we should take better care of our daughters, especially because they were girls.

More than I can say, we really worked hard. It got a little better later, but until then, we often worked with empty stomachs because there was always so much work to do.

I managed the hotel until my husband quit working for the Parises. My husband worked there for about a year and a half. I was so busy he had to help me wash sheets and pillowcases, and help the cook. Of course, he was very good at cooking. We cooked American and Japanese food, and sometimes had a mixed menu. I just had to make do with whatever I had. Sometimes I prepared fish, *nishime*, and *kōkō*, or pickled vegetables. And *miso,* or soybean paste, soup. People used to say, "Good food," when they ate at the hotel after coming back from work.

In the 1930s, business was pretty good. Those order-takers used to come. They used to write down what day of what month they would return, and how long their stay would be, on the office blackboard right before they left. We would reserve rooms accordingly. They were almost always the same people, except when a company sent a different order-taker, or when an order-taker quit, and a new one took over. I could manage the hotel with only those order-takers; we didn't need new customers. Sometimes we didn't have enough rooms when people travelling around the island came. But ten rooms were usually enough to put up all the order-takers and others. We used to let people sleep in our rooms when we didn't have an empty room. I don't remember whether it was then or not, but anyway, when a lot of order-takers came at the same time, we put *futon* on *goza* on the floor, not to mention using our boys' and girls' rooms. We had a lot of order-takers coming, and our business started to grow again.

But when World War II started, we had to close it to the public. We couldn't do anything. I don't know how the soldiers and heavy equipment came from America; but they were out there with the sounds of big trucks and cannon passing in front of our house in the dark. After they occupied Konawaena School everything was used by them. The generals asked us to feed the soldiers when they came to the hotel, since they didn't have any other place to go when they were off duty or didn't want to eat at the camp. They asked us to serve the soldiers first when they came to eat. This general said we could get as much food as we needed from either Theo H. Davies or American Factors and gave me a permit to order the food.

T-bone steaks were so cheap at the hotel that lots of people came, even from Waimea, when they were off duty. The only thing I worried about was the girls who worked for me. I was always watching them to see if they were bothered by soldiers. The girls were all Japanese, and I didn't want them to get hurt. I really had to watch them, since the soldiers were always asking for girls. Later, the Japanese girls quit because they were afraid of the Americans. So we hired Hawaiians who liked soldiers. They came in the morning and went home at night. Some *kanaka* girls stayed over.

At that time, lots of *kanaka* made money. Those who sold hot *shōchū,* low-grade distilled spirits, in Coca-Cola bottles in front of our hotel made money. They sold diluted ones for three to five dollars. Some, I think, drank a mixture of gasoline, or alcohol, and Coca-Cola. It was during the war, you know.

During those years, we couldn't take any local customers. People from this area could only go as far as Honaunau. We weren't allowed to go beyond that, and in the other direction, Kailua, Kona was as far as we could go. So we couldn't go anyplace. But there were lots of soldiers who had furloughs in Honolulu. They got furloughs after fighting and being in the army for some time, you know. Some wanted to see the other islands. And there were others who were having days off, or who had been transferred. After they arrived in Hilo, they would come to our place, since we were halfway between Hilo and Honolulu. They would come in a five-cent fare bus, all twelve of them, and stay at our hotel overnight; and next morning, they'd go on to their destinations. When one group left, another group would arrive; people were coming and going all the time.

The military wanted to have a contract with us. Since we didn't have any other customers, we signed the contract. They sent a person, a boss, who took charge of the accounting. He paid us according to what they owed, for dinner, breakfast, and any other meal. So our business started to grow again.

And we made enough money to pay the contractor, Yamane-*san,* who remodeled our hotel before the war. We paid back the money with some interest as well. As for Theo H. Davies, the lumber debt, we paid that little by little, monthly, from the money we saved. So, although we lost our regular business because of the war, it gave us soldiers; and we could make a lot of money, thanks to them.

Even after the war, since there were still quite a few soldiers coming in and out, we were doing okay. The community was growing; there were a lot of houses being built. Many order-takers came, and our business grew. Three of my children went to the war, including the one who is a dentist. When the one who'd been working in America came home —and was going to college in Honolulu then—we changed the ownership of the hotel to his name, Harold Manago; it would have been confiscated if it were in our name, since we were Japan-born. He became a teacher after graduating, thinking he wouldn't be drafted if he became a teacher. But he was drafted. He joined the military, leaving his wife and their two-month-old baby. The dentist son went to Italy the other one went to France, and the third one went to America. You know those internment camps for Japanese, he was helping there, teaching English to the old people. After the war, they all came home to help the hotel. Now, my son, Harold, and grandson, Dwight, manage the hotel.

Looking back on my life, I now think Hawaii must have been good luck for me, although there were some difficult times. It's amazing we could work so hard. My husband and I must have been made out of steel, we both have been so healthy. We brought up our children unspoiled; all my children worked hard, picking coffee, cutting firewood, doing laundry, ironing and cleaning, and helping me. I would hear about new movie theaters being built, but we didn't go even once in the first fifteen years. That's how hard we worked. It's hard to believe what we did in those days, but . . . that's my real history.

Glossary

Language appears in brackets following the word. "Pidgin" indicates one of a variety of pidgin languages spoken in Hawaii or Hawaiian Creole.

'ae [Hawaiian]   Yes.
'ahi [Hawaiian]   Hawaiian tuna fishes, especially the yellow-fin tuna.
'ahina [Hawaiian]   Blue denim cloth.
aikāne [Hawaiian]   Friend.
'āina [Hawaiian]   Land, earth.
akamai [Hawaiian]   Smart, clever, expert.
aku [Hawaiian]   Bonito, skipjack.
akule [Hawaiian]   Big-eyed or goggle-eyed scad fish.

bagoong [Filipino]   Salty small fish or shrimp relish. In this context, used as a derogatory term of address.
bandorya [Filipino]   Mandolin, a musical instrument.
bangō [Japanese]   Number. In this context, used to mean an employee identification number or employee identification number tag.
batan [Japanese]   Bang!
bayaw [Filipino]   Brother-in-law. In this context, used as a derogatory term of address.
bentō [Japanese]   Lunch.

chee [Pidgin]   Mild exclamation.
cowboy or *koboy* [Filipino]   Literally, "cowboy." In this context, used to mean an abductor of women. —*cowboy-cowboy* or *koboy-koboy* Practice of abducting women.

da kine [Pidgin] An expression with an unspecified referent; "whatchamacallit".

daikon [Japanese] Pickled radish.

dango [Japanese] Dumpling.

furo [Japanese] A public bath; a bathtub, heated from underneath.

futon [Japanese] A thick bed quilt.

gaijin [Japanese] A foreigner.

ganzume [Japanese] A coal-trimming rake.

gari-gari [Japanese] A scratching sound.

goro-goro-goro [Japanese] A rumbling sound.

goza [Japanese] A mat.

gun [Japanese] A sub-prefecture.

ha [Hawaiian] Breath, life.

hali'i [Hawaiian] To spread, as a sheet.

hanahana [Pidgin] Work, labor.

haole [Hawaiian] Caucasian; foreigner.

hapa haole [Hawaiian] Part-Caucasian.

hāpai [Hawaiian] To carry.

hāwa'e [Hawaiian] A sea urchin.

hilot [Filipino] Literally, "to massage, as a sprain." In this context, used to mean folk healer.

hō hana [Hawaiian] Literally, "hoe work"; weeding.

ho'oponopono [Hawaiian] Mental cleansing; the old Hawaiian method of clearing the mind of a sick person by family discussion, examination, and prayer.

hoy [Filipino] An exclamation of warning or calling attention.

hui [Hawaiian] Association.

hukilau [Hawaiian] To fish with the seine.

huli [Hawaiian] Taro top, as used for planting.

'ina [Hawaiian] Young of the sea urchin.

jii-san [Japanese] Old man.

kahuna [Hawaiian] Priest, minister, sorcerer, expert in any profession.

kālai [Hawaiian] To cut sugar cane.

kanaka [Hawaiian] Hawaiian person.

kanakē [Hawaiian] Candy.

kasuri [Japanese] Cloth with splashed patterns.

katsuo-bushi [Japanese] Dried bonito.

kaukau [Pidgin] Food.

ke [Hawaiian]   The.
keiki [Hawaiian]   Shoot, as of taro.
kekkon [Japanese]   Marriage.
ken [Japanese]   A prefecture.
kiawe [Hawaiian]   Algaroba tree.
kin [Japanese]   1.323 lbs.
kōkō [Japanese]   Pickled vegetables.
kōkua [Hawaiian]   To help, assist, support.
kōkua luna [Hawaiian]   Assistant foreman.
kompadre [Filipino]   The address used reciprocally between the parents of a
   child and the child's godfather.
kompang [Pidgin]   Sugar cane cultivation by a small group.
koshimaki [Japanese]   An underskirt.
kūkae [Hawaiian]   Excreta.
kukui [Hawaiian]   Candlenut tree.
kūō [Hawaiian]   To cry loudly.
kuruma-fu [Japanese]   Wheel-shaped wheat-gluten bread.

lau hala [Hawaiian]   Pandanus leaf, especially as used in plaiting.
limu [Hawaiian]   A general name for all kinds of plants living under water.
luna [Hawaiian]   Foreman.

mana [Hawaiian]   Supernatural or divine power.
manapua See "mea'ono-pua'a."
manju [Japanese]   Bun with bean-jam filling.
manong [Filipino]   An older brother; an older man. In this context, may be
   used to mean someone of Filipino ancestry; also used as a derogatory
   term of address.
mea [Hawaiian]   Thing.
mea'ono-pua'a [Hawaiian]   Chinese pork cake.
miso [Japanese]   Soybean paste.
mochi [Japanese]   Rice cake.
montsuki [Japanese]   A crested kimono.
mo'opuna [Hawaiian]   Grandchild.
mura [Japanese]   A village.
mushiro [Japanese]   A straw mat.

Naichi [Japanese]   Japanese from the main islands of Japan.
namasu [Japanese]   A dish of vegetables seasoned in vinegar.
nishime [Japanese]   A dish of vegetables boiled with soy sauce.
nui [Hawaiian]   Big.

oba-san-tachi [Japanese]   Literally, "aunties." In this context, used to refer to
   a trio of matrons.

obi [Japanese]   A sash.

'ōkole [Hawaiian]   Literally, "buttocks." Chinese cake stuffed with meat, named for a resemblance to buttocks.

'ōkolehao [Hawaiian]   Literally, "iron bottom." Liquor distilled from *tī* root.

'ole [Hawaiian]   Not, without, lacking.

'ono [Hawaiian]   Delicious.

'ōpae [Hawaiian]   General name for shrimp.

'ōpelu [Hawaiian]   Mackerel scad.

'opihi [Hawaiian]   Limpet.

pahu-puhi paka [Hawaiian]   Tobacco box.

pa'i a'i [Hawaiian]   Heavy, as poorly made cake.

Pake [Hawaiian]   Chinese.

pata-pata-pata [Japanese]   Pattering.

pau [Hawaiian]   Finished.

pepeiao [Hawaiian]   Literally, "ear." Chinese cake stuffed with meat, named for a resemblance to an ear.

piko [Hawaiian]   Navel.

pilut [Pidgin]   Drunkard.

poi [Hawaiian]   Hawaiian staff of life, made from cooked taro corms, pounded and thinned with water.

pōpolo [Hawaiian]   Black nightshade, a weed with small black edible berries.

pua'a [Hawaiian]   Pork.

puka [Hawaiian]   Hole.

ri [Japanese]   2.44 miles.

saimin [Pidgin]   Noodle dish.

sakada [Filipino]   Laborers sent out of their native place.

sakazuki [Japanese]   Ceremony of exchanging nuptial cups.

sake [Japanese]   Alcoholic drink.

salalabit [Pidgin]   Derogatory term of address.

-san [Japanese]   Mr., Mrs., Ms.

sara-sara [Japanese]   Rustling sound.

sensei [Japanese]   Teacher.

shake tin [Japanese and English]   Literally, "salmon tin." Canned salmon.

shashin kekkon [Japanese]   A long-distance arranged marriage based on an exchange of photographs.

shee [Pidgin]   Mild exclamation.

shibori [Japanese]   A white-spotted cloth.

shimpai [Japanese]   Literally, "look after." Arrange a marriage.

shinbo shitara [Japanese]   Literally, "If I persevered . . ."

shingenbukuro [Japanese]   A cloth pouch.

shiri [Japanese]   Buttocks.

shirimochi [Japanese]   Manure.

shizoku [Japanese]   A descendant of a samurai.
shōchū [Japanese]   Low-class distilled spirits.
shōyu [Japanese]   Soy sauce.
son [Japanese]   Village.
sumō [Japanese]   Japanese wrestling.

takuan [Japanese]   Pickled radish.
tanomoshi [Japanese]   Mutual financing association.
tatami [Japanese]   Straw matting, about three by six feet.
tī [Tahitian and Maori]   A woody plant *(Cordyline terminalis)* in the lily family, found from tropical Asia eastward to Hawaii.
ton-ton [Japanese]   A knocking sound.
tūtū [Hawaiian]   Grandparent.

udon [Japanese]   Noodles.
'uha-loa [Hawaiian]   A small weed, whose leaves and inner bark are used for tea or chewed to relieve sore throat.
ulua [Hawaiian]   Certain species of crevalle or jack, a game fish.
ume [Japanese]   Pickled plum.

wana [Hawaiian]   A sea urchin.
wen [Pidgin]   Past tense indicator.
won bok [Chinese]   Chinese cabbage.

-ya [Japanese]   Shop; store; place.
yanagi-gōri [Japanese]   Wicker trunk.
yōshi [Japanese]   A son-in-law adopted into his wife's family.

zori [Japanese]   Sandals.

SOURCES

Ernesto Constantino, *Ilokano Dictionary* (Honolulu: University Press of Hawaii, 1976).

Koh Masuda, *Kenkyusha's New Japanese-English Dictionary* (Tokyo: Kenkyusha, 1974).

Mary Kawena Pukui and Samuel H. Elbert, *Hawaiian Dictionary* (Honolulu: University Press of Hawaii, 1977).

Teresita V. Ramos, *Tagalog Dictionary* (Honolulu: University Press of Hawaii, 1975).

Elsa P. Yap and Maria V. R. Bunye, *Cebuano-Visayan Dictionary* (Honolulu: University of Hawaii Press, 1971).

Additional definitions were provided by interviewers and interviewees.

INDEX

Index was compiled by Katharine Kan, MLS.